UNTANGLING

CALLUNA PRESS

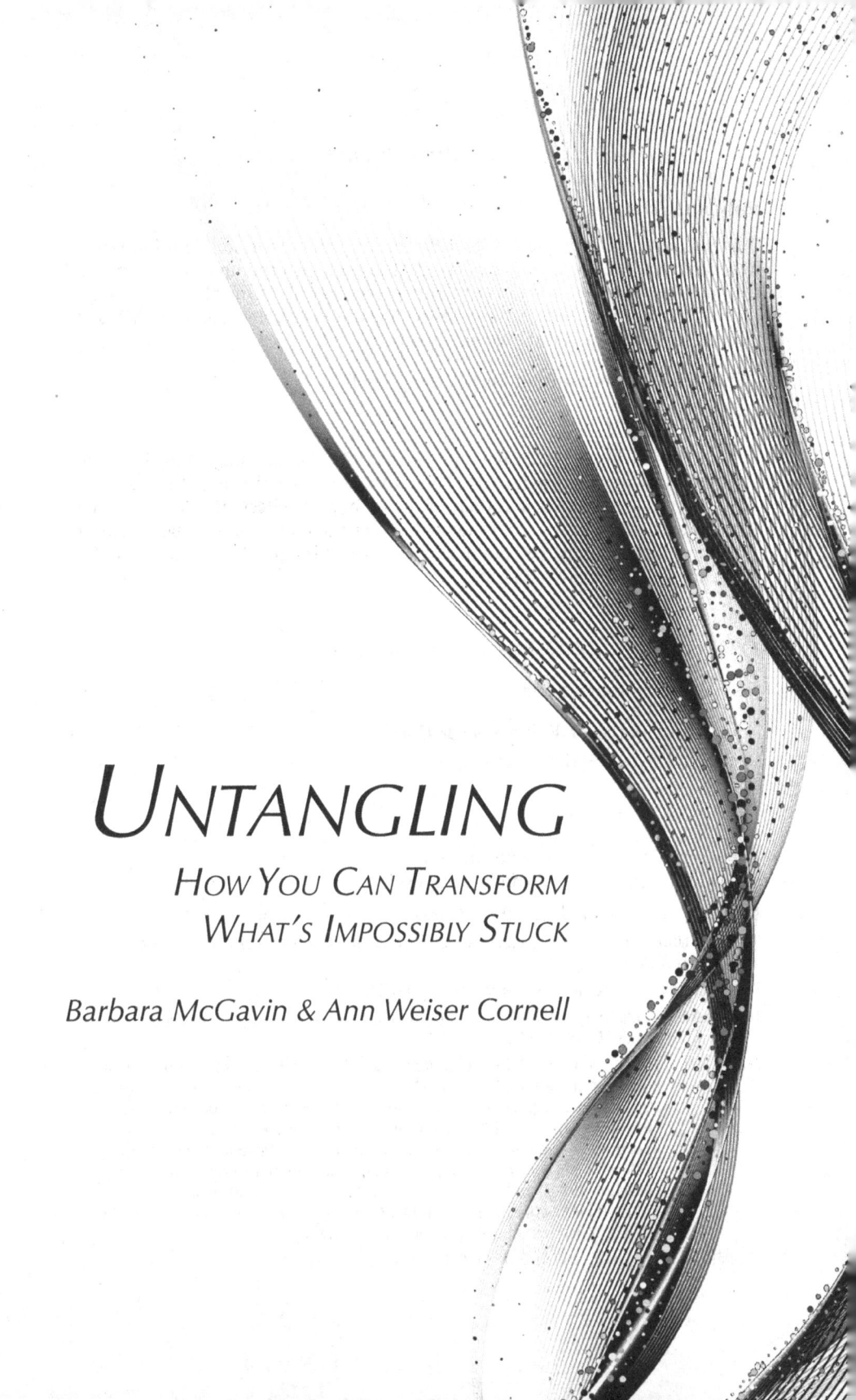

UNTANGLING

How You Can Transform What's Impossibly Stuck

Barbara McGavin & Ann Weiser Cornell

For our students

Publisher's Note

This publication is designed to provide accurate and authoritative information in regard to the subject matter covered. It is sold with the understanding that the publisher is not engaged in rendering psychological, financial, legal, or other professional services. If expert assistance or counseling is needed, the services of a competent professional should be sought.

© 2024 Barbara McGavin and Ann Weiser Cornell

All rights reserved

In accordance with the U.S. Copyright Act of 1976, the scanning, uploading, and electronic sharing of any part of this book without the permission of the publisher constitute unlawful piracy and theft of the authors' intellectual property. If you would like to use material from the book (other than for review purposes), prior written permission must be obtained by contacting the publisher. Thank you for your support of the authors' rights.

Calluna Press
1474 University Ave, #155, Berkeley, CA 94702 USA

www.focusingresources.com

Cover image and cover design: Maggie Hurley
Design and layout: Barbara McGavin

Publisher's Cataloging-in-Publication
(Provided by Cassidy Cataloguing Services, Inc.).

Names:	McGavin, Barbara, author.	Cornell, Ann Weiser, author.
Title:	Untangling : how you can transform what's impossibly stuck / Barbara McGavin & Ann Weiser Cornell.
Description:	Berkeley, CA : Calluna Press, [2024]
Identifiers:	ISBN: 979-8-9905392-0-4 (paperback)	978-0-9721058-6-6 (ebook)	LCCN: 2024908584
Subjects:	LCSH: Problem solving--Popular works.	Personality change--Popular works.	Self- actualization (Psychology)--Popular works.	Compulsive behavior--Psychological aspects--Popular works.	Compulsive behavior--Treatment--Popular works.	Anxiety-- Treatment--Popular works.	Self-doubt--Treatment--Popular works.	Substance abuse-- Treatment--Popular works.	Perfectionism (Personality trait)--Treatment--Popular works.	Mindfulness (Psychology)--Popular works.	LCGFT: Self-help publications.	BISAC: SELF-HELP / General.	SELF-HELP / Compulsive Behavior / General.	SELF-HELP / Substance Abuse & Addictions / General.
Classification:	LCC: BF698.2 .M34 2024	DDC: 155.25--dc23

Contents

Preface	1
PART ONE: UNTANGLING	**9**
Chapter 1 How it All Began	11
Chapter 2 It's a Tangle	17
Chapter 3 Tangled Up in Parts	29
PART TWO: ALL TANGLED UP	**39**
Chapter 4 Hijack	41
Chapter 5 Takeover	49
Chapter 6 Rebellion	55
Chapter 7 Intimidation	63
Chapter 8 Despair	71
Chapter 9 Longing	77
PART THREE: THE POWERS OF PRESENCE	**87**
Chapter 10 The Environment of Transformation	89
Chapter 11 Becoming Your Biggest Self	95
Chapter 12 Always Room for One More	115
Chapter 13 The Magic of Empathy	125
Chapter 14 A Tale of Two Parts	141
Chapter 15 The Healing Power of Love	151
Chapter 16 Last-Ditch Efforts	161
Chapter 17 The Thawing of the Frozen Core	175
Chapter 18 Widening the Horizon	183
PART FOUR: LIVING FREE	**193**
Chapter 19 Life Emerging	195
Chapter 20 Living Beyond Tangles	203
APPENDIX	**217**
Some Untangling terms	218
Some books that influenced us	221
Ways to go further	223
With Gratitude and Appreciation	225

Every bad feeling is potential energy toward a more right way of being, if you give it space to move toward its rightness.

Eugene Gendlin, *Focusing*, p. 76.

Preface

Our careers, our relationships, and our happiness were on the line. Even though we were experienced workshop leaders—even though other people looked to us for help—we were each secretly facing some of the biggest, toughest, most problematic issues of our lives.

Ann was drinking too much—more and more often. Barbara sometimes felt so inadequate and worthless that she thought she'd be better off disappearing—permanently. We both felt deeply ashamed about having these problems, and we were doing our utmost to pretend they didn't exist.

The first inkling of a breakthrough came when we confessed to each other what we were struggling with. The method we had been teaching (Focusing) had helped us in many ways, but these entrenched problems had remained untouched. We realized there and then that we needed to find a way to bring real change.

Pooling our resources, and building on what we'd each already been developing, we found ourselves creating entirely new processes. And, of course, we were trying them out first for ourselves.

They worked. Ann stopped drinking, and Barbara stopped wanting to disappear. What a relief!

These were huge changes. But something else happened that turned out to be even more important.

It turned out that we didn't have to "fix" ourselves or "solve" our problems. When we saw our problematic issues as defects or failures, we were stuck with them. When we treated ourselves with radical empathy and self-acceptance, the problems quite literally solved themselves.

Since then, our lives have changed in remarkable and often surprising ways, and so have the lives of hundreds of our students. For the past thirty years, we've been wanting to write a book to share what we have learned. Thanks to the pandemic and a lot of hard work, we now have one.

With this book, we offer our method to you. If this book helps you have greater compassion for what you have been struggling with in your life, greater confidence to face what is challenging, and greater freedom to live a satisfying and fulfilling life, we're delighted.

Before we dive into sharing our Untangling method with you, we'd like to give you a bit of background. There are two methods which have formed the foundation for Untangling: Focusing, and Inner Relationship Focusing.

Focusing

Focusing was developed in the 1950s by Eugene Gendlin, from research into change in psychotherapy at the University of Chicago. This research showed that clients who were significantly more successful did something that could be easily observed, even in the first few sessions. They slowed down, pausing to sense something inside themselves. They hesitated, groping for the words that would fit this bodily-felt experience. Gendlin called this "getting a felt sense."

The Focusing method involves deliberately inviting a felt sense of something (for example: a problem, a situation, a person, how your life is going right now, or even a work of art) and then spending time with it. To do Focusing, you bring to mind what you want to have a felt sense of, and you sense in the middle area of your body—primarily in your throat, chest, and stomach—and be as friendly, open, and curious as you can toward whatever you feel. When you get a sense of something, the next step is to find descriptions and symbols for what is felt. Checking those descriptions with what you are sensing in your body until they match, is a key aspect of the process.

When the felt sense and the words or other symbols match, a felt shift happens. You may have insights that illuminate something that may have been puzzling or troubling you. Your body feels different—more relaxed, more at ease, more open.

Focusing is practiced primarily as a self-help skill, in peer partnerships or on one's own. It is used in a wide range of circumstances: for emotional healing, to enhance spirituality and creativity, to help ease the suffering of chronic pain and illness, and in many other areas of life.

It has been combined with a wide range of psychotherapy, counseling, and coaching modalities by hundreds of therapists and counselors worldwide, as well as offered in guided sessions by trained Focusing Practitioners.

Inner Relationship Focusing

As soon as we met in 1991, it became clear that we had been working in parallel to elaborate and extend aspects of Gendlin's work centering on the "inner relationship" in Focusing. Once we joined forces, progress on this approach advanced more rapidly.

We independently discovered that sometimes it isn't easy to get a felt sense. We observed how people often got caught up in emotional reactions or endless thoughts. We found that when people develop an inner relationship with those reactions and thoughts, it makes a difference in being able to have a felt sense. Developing an inner relationship with partial selves (Parts) frees a person to be able to connect with this deeper, more subtle level of meaning.

Inner Relationship Focusing (IRF) is our own development of Focusing. We have trained many students in this method, as well as writing a manual on it, The Focusing Student's and Companion's Manual (2002), that is used worldwide today. Wikipedia calls IRF "the commonest adaptation of the Focusing form used today."

IRF emphasizes the quality of the relationship between the "I" of the whole self and the "it" of a Part. For emotional healing to happen, this needs to be a relationship of acceptance, empathy, compassion, and even love.

Untangling

It was three years after we began working together, on our way to teach an IRF workshop, that Ann was forced to confront the way she was using alcohol. The question was whether the principles of IRF could help—or could be made to help—with something as serious and difficult as this. The answer: "Yes... and."

Yes, IRF could help. And it needed to be enhanced, refined, and developed. Coming to grips with the most difficult life issues either of us had ever faced required new concepts and methods. To develop them, we drew further on the work of Eugene Gendlin.

Gendlin was not only a psychotherapist, he was a philosopher who created a model of what it means to be a living being with other living beings, how things get stuck and how they can change at their most fundamental levels. His remarkable Philosophy of the Implicit is at the heart of Untangling. Our new methods, based on Gendlin's philosophy, opened up whole vistas of how to understand and resolve some of the toughest human "tangles."

What this book is not

We don't promise to heal all ills. We can't even be sure our method will help you, although we think it's likely. We definitely don't think we offer the only thing that helps. There are many other methods out there that have helped many people, and we are honored to join them rather than claiming to replace them. We invite you to be responsible, self-aware, and guided by your own inner sense of rightness.

Being gentle with yourself while reading this book

Coming to terms with issues that may have affected much of your life can bring up strong feelings. Emotions may be triggered. You may see aspects of yourself that you were not aware of until now. Parts of you might be upset or ashamed about what you discover.

If you are struggling with the kind of issues this book can help with, you are quite likely to be reading with certain biases from the start. You'll almost certainly have a side of you that's reading to find out what's wrong with you, convinced there is something flawed about you that you need to be shamed and criticized into changing. You're likely to also have a side of you that resists being changed and is ready to undermine and refuse anything that pushes it. All this is natural.

However, nothing in this book is meant to criticize you. We hope to show you how everything in you has been doing its best to help you. We invite you to read with curiosity and generosity toward yourself, because you are more than something in you that harshly judges or something in you that feels resentful or acts like an impulsive child. You are your wise, spacious, whole self—even when that feels like a fantasy.

Read slowly, and take breaks when you need to. Read with a good friend and talk about what's being stirred up. Write in a journal. Meditate. Take walks. Doing whatever nourishes you will make going further and deeper more possible. You may also want to have more support by working with

Preface

a counselor, therapist, or Focusing facilitator in conjunction with your Untangling process.

And keep reading. By the end of the book you will know that Untangling itself generates the resources you need in order not to be hijacked or taken over by the Parts that have entangled your life until now. There is hope. There is life beyond Tangles.

Part One
Untangling

Nothing that feels bad is ever the last step.

Eugene Gendlin, *Focusing,* p. 26

You know those problems in your life that you think are the worst, the most despicable, the biggest, most utterly insoluble? Those are the places where your greatest growth and transformation are waiting to happen.

Yes, the very place that seems to be such an intractable problem holds within itself everything needed for it to resolve. It does need you to bring a certain kind of awareness to it, but it absolutely doesn't require you to fix or figure out or force anything to change. As a matter of fact, trying to fix or force or figure it out will only keep things stuck.

Wherever there is something that is impossible to think or feel or do in your life, you are finding the exact spot where the next step in your life is still ready, waiting to happen. It doesn't matter how long ago it got all jammed up. The right next step of your life can still happen.

When you know that transformation happens where something in your life feels impossible, it becomes possible to lean toward what feels bad. You can turn toward it, gather it to you, listen to it, love it. The place that seems so hopelessly stuck will untangle itself when you give it the attention it needs.

What is the attention it needs and how do you provide it? That's what this book is about.

Part One: Untangling

Chapter 1
How it All Began

It was September 1994, and we—Barbara and Ann—were about to lead several Focusing workshops in the softly rolling hills of Devon, England, and the lush green of County Wicklow, Ireland. We had become friends through our shared interest in Focusing, and now we were going to teach together. But there were some important things we didn't know about each other.

Ann didn't know that clever, competent Barbara struggled with feeling hopelessly inadequate and inferior no matter what she accomplished. She didn't know Barbara lived in fear of being knocked off her precarious perch by debilitating depression and excoriating self-criticism.

Barbara didn't know that cheerful, friendly Ann was getting drunk three or four nights a week and telling herself that this was normal, while at the same time anxiously worrying about whether she might actually have a serious problem.

We each struggled silently and not very successfully with these painful issues, even though, as international experts in a healing personal growth process, we were supposed to have our own lives pretty well in order.

But soon, for both of us, everything was going to change...

ANN: On September 12, 1994, the very first thing I did when I got off the flight from California to England was to buy a bottle of wine. I made my way to Bath, where Barbara and I met up and had dinner together, and then I said I needed an early night. I lied. The truth was that I wanted to get back to my room at the B&B and be alone with my wine. By the time I went to bed, the bottle was two-thirds empty.

The next day, Barbara took me on a sightseeing trip to the nearby city of Wells. The cathedral was magnificent, and the area around it was charming. As we were walking back to the car, we passed a community theater at the edge of town. I pointed out to Barbara

Part One: Untangling

that they were putting on *Trial by Jury* and *The Pirates of Penzance*, my two favorite operettas by Gilbert and Sullivan.

But I couldn't even imagine that I could come back to Wells later to see them. Instead, as we passed a wine store, I excused myself and went in to buy another bottle.

The following morning I was on my own. I decided to go to Glastonbury. I walked on the Tor, visited the ruined abbey where King Arthur and Queen Guinevere are said to be buried, and sat by the Chalice Well. It was a lovely day.

After lunch, a voice in my head started up, saying, "Now let's get back to the room and drink." Another voice countered it with disagreements and anxious worries. They made a familiar cacophony, those two voices—an argument that could only be silenced by getting drunk.

Trying to escape from that inner argument, I found myself in a bookstore. Unusually for me, I roamed the aisles restlessly, not seeing any book that attracted me. When my eye fell on a book about alcoholism, I picked it up. As I turned to its self-diagnosis questionnaire, my thought was, "I'll prove to myself I'm not an alcoholic—and then I can go to my room and drink in peace."

I started down the list of questions... and I saw myself in every word. *Do you buy ahead to protect the supply?* Um, yes. *Do you gulp to get high faster?* Yes to that too. *Obsessing about drinking?* Just what I'm doing right now. *Drinking alone so that no human relationship would get in the way of my relationship with the alcohol?* I had to answer yes to every question.

I stood in the bookstore with my whole life spinning around me. The argument had ended. Now what was I going to do? I couldn't just go back to my room and drink. But it felt like I had lost my best friend, and I had no idea what would take its place.

Then I had a wild notion. It was almost as if the idea came from another version of me. "If I were a different person," it went, "I would figure out a way to go to Wells and see those Gilbert and Sullivan plays."

And that is what I did. By 8 PM I was in Wells, filled with delight and joy, watching the plays I love performed with all the verve and spirit of a community troupe... and I wasn't missing drinking in my room at all. For the moment, it seemed I was free at last.

But as every person who is addicted to something knows, stopping is only the beginning.

The next day I woke up full of shame, uncertainty and doubt. Barbara and I drove to the retreat center near Exeter to teach the first of our workshops. I got up the courage to confess to her how often I had been drinking in the evening to get drunk, that now I had stopped, and that I felt terribly ashamed and untrusting of myself. I felt I had been fooling myself for years... and I wasn't quite sure anymore what to trust.

Barbara said, "Why don't we do some Focusing?"

BARBARA: When Ann told me what she was going through I was moved by the obvious pain she was in. Focusing hadn't made a difference with Ann's drinking, but it had helped in so many other areas of our lives. Maybe together we could discover how to make it work with this as well.

In every free moment when we weren't teaching—early morning, after lunch, in the evening—we traded Focusing sessions. After every session, I made notes on what I was noticing in our process. Each pattern I saw generated a host of further questions and avenues to explore.

Ann saying she had been fooling herself got me thinking. It's common to speak like that—"*I* have been fooling *myself*"—but really, *who* is fooling *whom*? Were there parts of her operating outside her awareness? I was pretty sure there was a part of her that still wanted to drink. Would it be a good idea for her to get to know that part better?

ANN: Barbara encouraged me to turn toward the part that wanted to drink. I could definitely feel it was still there. I started to realize there was also a part that was terribly anxious and wanted to control the drinking part, to lock it up and never let it see the light of day. There was also something else I could feel that wasn't either one of those parts. It was like some kind of "me." It felt like a "me" that could be an attentive and compassionate listener to each part without taking sides.

Part One: Untangling

Being an attentive and compassionate listener with both the part that wanted to drink *and* the part that wanted to control it, I was able to learn more about them.

I discovered that my drinking had started as a way to be close to my alcoholic father after he died, when I lacked the inner resources and support to grieve for him. It was also a way to numb and distract myself from the complicated feelings of grief for a father I still felt ambivalent about.

I also learned, to my surprise, that drinking was a way to access qualities that had been shut down in my childhood: being spontaneous, being creative, being sensual, being goofy. As a kid, I'd been scolded and shamed for my exuberant liveliness, so I'd covered it over with being "good," being cooperative, following the rules. Drinking was a way to break free for a few hours, but button everything up again the next day.

As Barbara and I continued to work together, I could feel myself being more expressive, more spontaneous, more exuberant, without needing to drink to get there. I was amazed. I thought that addressing my drinking issue would only bring more feelings of shame and humiliation, but I was actually becoming joyfully and fully myself.

It was like expecting to find coal in my Christmas stocking and instead finding jewels. There was treasure—the treasure of regaining my aliveness.

BARBARA: I found what we were doing absorbing and fascinating. I took the opportunity to do Focusing on my own tough stuff. I was sure there were hidden parts doing things in me too, and I wanted to know what was going on.

I remembered the inner work I had already done on my own suicidal depression, and how I had created a compassionate inner relationship with the part of me that wanted to die. I no longer felt the pull to escape my life through death.

But there were still times when I sank into a dark depression with a painful sense that I wasn't worth the space I was taking up. I knew I still needed to give more caring attention to those kinds of feelings in me. It would be great if that too could change.

Our sessions grew deeper and deeper. We found we needed to develop whole new ways of being with our confused and confusing parts. The work itself demanded a stronger and more precise kind of inner relationship. After every session, we would pull out our notebooks to capture what had happened and what we learned about our process.

When we engaged with our toughest issues, using everything we were learning, something started to happen. Whatever seemed to be an unbearable, shameful problem—wanting to drink or eat, feeling blocked about doing something, being obsessed with someone, feeling inadequate and useless—turned out to show precisely where the riches of our vibrant aliveness were to be found. It was like a treasure map.

The recovery of our inner treasure—our aliveness that had been frozen and abandoned—occurred over and over in those intensive few weeks.

Although we were already noticing some extraordinary changes in ourselves, it all felt new and not yet solid. We thought we should keep what we were finding to ourselves until we felt more sure about it. But our workshop participants kept asking us questions we could only answer by drawing on our newest discoveries. We would look at each other, wondering if we should say something, but it just didn't feel right to hold back what we were discovering, raw and incomplete as it was.

Our participants were eager for more and kept asking us when we would do a retreat on *this* work. By the following summer, we held our first workshop based on these new discoveries. We called it *Treasure Maps to the Soul*.

We also started writing this book. But there was so much we didn't yet know. We needed to teach and work with others, do our own work, and learn a lot more before we would be ready to share it with the rest of the world.

Over the years, we started to call impossibly difficult life issues *Tangles*. Hence we call the method we developed for engaging with those issues *Untangling*.

We have created a theoretical model to describe what is happening in Tangles, but the theory didn't come first. Experiential process—ours and our students'—came first.

Our amazing and courageous students have given us many rich opportunities to develop the Untangling method and theory. At every workshop we continue to learn so much more about what Tangles are, how they form and how they can untangle.

Part One: Untangling

In this book, you will find stories of what we did and how we changed. Ann's struggle with drinking is now far in the past, and so are other Tangles that turned out to be connected with that: a block to being authentic and a terror of interpersonal conflict. Today, she feels a calm, balanced confidence in just about all situations, even the tough ones. Barbara no longer falls into dark depressions. Her self-criticism has faded away so much it is hard for her to even remember the last time she was hard on herself. She moves through her days with curiosity, openness, and a willingness to be present to whatever occurs.

Life continues to be more and more fun and flowing for both of us, every year. It has greater challenges as well as accomplishments. Above all, our connections with others have become much richer and more rewarding.

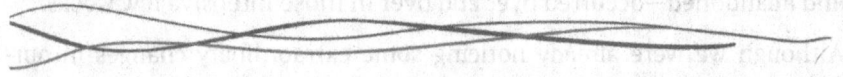

Here is our message to you: By turning toward the most hopelessly stuck and painful parts of your life with compassion and curiosity, you can live more courageously, creatively and authentically.

That's what happened for us. It's what we want for you. In the rest of this book, we will show you how.

Chapter 2
IT'S A TANGLE

BARBARA: Since my early teens, one area of my life was excruciatingly difficult, painful and full of shame. It was the struggle over my weight.

When I was a kid, I was so thin my aunt said I looked "delicate." I ate whatever I wanted without even thinking about it. Then when I was twelve I started to put on weight. I didn't like that, but I assumed it was just part of becoming a teenager.

By the time I was fourteen I was overweight and living smack-dab in the middle of an inner war. Since then there have been skirmishes, battles, negotiations, periods of relative calm and times when full-blown conflict was raging. I lost weight, and gained it, lost it, and gained it over and over... and as the years went by, my weight kept creeping up and up. I felt disgusted and sick and ashamed every time I stood on the scales.

I wore clothes carefully chosen to camouflage my size. I always hid behind something or someone when photos were being taken. I hid my scales and went to Big Is Beautiful workshops. I felt resentful of those skinny people who seemed to be able to eat whatever they wanted without gaining an ounce. I longed to stop feeling like I was engaged in a never-ending battle about food.

By the time I was more than fifty pounds overweight, I was frantic to control what, when and how much I ate. I would go for weeks trying my best to be "good," while another part of me hidden in the shadows felt increasingly rebellious and resentful. Until I was upset by something—maybe I felt criticized or overwhelmed or sad or depressed—and I'd find myself eating the stale chocolate hidden in the back of the cupboard and the cold potatoes left on my daughter's plate, and sneaking an extra helping of dessert. I wasn't particularly discriminating about what I ate as long as it went into

Part One: Untangling

my mouth as quickly as possible and numbed my feelings into a grey quiet.

The "I'm going to be good" side would have the upper hand for a while, but the other side bided its time in the background, like the forces of the Resistance, just waiting for a moment to blow up the bridge and take over again.

The fighting between the different sides could be ferocious. It often seemed that the only way to resolve this conflict would be to choose one side and get rid of the other. Of course, *that* didn't work.

This situation went on for years with no relief or resolution.

Perpetually stuck

ANN: I have always wanted to be a writer.

When I was young, I wrote a lot. When I was six, I created little books of stories. When I was thirteen, if the assignment was to write one sentence for each of the week's vocabulary words, I used the words to write a story instead. When I was fifteen, I was well into my first novel.

But then something mysterious happened. My writing dried up.

If I had an assignment for school, I would procrastinate until the night before and then force myself to stay up and do it, a procedure that felt as painful as pulling teeth. Writing was no longer fun.

And yet... the longing to write something that touched and moved people did not go away. I managed to get through school, and in the years that followed, the longing crystalized into the determination to write a book. I felt that if I could write a book, I could help change the world in a positive direction. There wasn't anything I wanted more.

But it didn't happen. I would write a bit, and then stop. Months later, write a bit, stop again. Occasionally I would get a burst of writing fervor that would last for weeks. But it would always grind to a halt.

I started to wonder if there was something wrong with me. Maybe I was deficient in some way, just not good enough somehow. That made it worse: every time I started trying to write again, I carried with me the burden of my past failures.

I called it my "writer's block" and tried all sorts of things to cure it. I made a deal to meet with a friend every morning, talk about our writing, and then move to separate rooms to write. She wrote her paper. I didn't write my book.

I tried different schedules, waking up earlier, moving my desk to a different place in the house. I'd feel hopeful because these new arrangements would work—until they didn't.

I tried accepting that this was simply how things were and I'd better just get used to it. I wasn't ever going to be a writer. I wasn't ever going to write a book.

And yet the longing was still there. I could tell myself to give up, but giving up didn't work either. The part of me that wanted to give up and the part of me that didn't want to give up were at odds with each other, and neither one was backing down.

I felt frustrated, defeated, and defective. Many aspects of life went on, but this aspect of my life stayed stuck. Years went by.

It was a Tangle

Ann had a problem with alcohol, and Barbara had a problem with food. Ann had writer's block, and Barbara had suicidal depression. (And we had other issues as well, as you will discover.)

You can find many books on depression, or on alcohol or eating issues, or on procrastination and writer's block, as if all of them are separate kinds of problems. But here is the insight that shifted everything for us: *These are all the same kind of problem.*

We call it a *Tangle*.

If you want to do something that you should be able to do, but it feels *impossible*—like Ann wanting to write—you are caught in a Tangle. Maybe you find it impossible to stop doing something—like Barbara and her struggles with food—that's also a Tangle. Or it might be impossible to believe you have what it takes to accomplish something. Or it might seem impossible to feel safe even when there is nothing apparently threatening you.

Part One: Untangling

Are Tangles just difficult problems?

Every day we experience problems. We *need* problems that challenge us. Challenges are an opportunity for growth and creativity. They call for us to develop our abilities and resources. We learn from our challenges.

Any interruption in the flow of life can call on your ingenuity and persistence. You spill the milk, you go to clean up the milk. Oops, you're out of paper towels and you don't want to use the dish sponge on the floor. Okay, so you go buy paper towels, or use toilet paper, or pull a dirty shirt out of the laundry and use that.

Obviously there are plenty of problems that are much more complicated than cleaning up spilled milk. They take time and thought and require significant resources. Moving house is one of the more challenging situations most of us face at one time or another. You imagine what kind of place you want and what you need. You look at places, you make lists of pros and cons, you figure out how you're going to pay for it, and so on... But it's still a relatively straightforward problem.

Whether it's sorting out your taxes or getting to the Moon, difficult problems are soluble if you have the right resources. You can use your experience and knowledge, gut instinct, intellect, support from others, experimentation, and so on to find a way to deal with them. That's how you know they're not *Tangles*.

So what is a Tangle?

A Tangle is a kind of problem that is complex in a fiendish kind of way. It is, in some fundamental way, impossible to solve. Whoa! What did we just say? That's right. If you try to solve the Tangle *from inside itself*, it is impossible to solve.

Before you throw this book across the room in disgust, we want to reassure you that Tangles can and do untangle.

It might be relieving to know the reason you're feeling stuck, the reason your problem has been so intractable, is *not* that you are stupid or lazy or crazy. The problem lies within the structure of the Tangle itself.

A Tangle is a type of problem that cannot be solved at the level of what it seems to be about. For example, you'd think that if the problem is about exercising, all you'd need to do is figure out a way to get yourself to the gym or out the door for a bike ride or a walk. If this is a Tangle, even if you do get to the gym every single day, it won't solve your Tangle. (It would be nice if it would, but it won't.)

No matter how smart or determined or disciplined you are, when you are caught up in a Tangle you are living inside an emotional and cognitive boundary that limits even what you are able to *perceive*. It's like growing up on an island in the middle of an ocean with no way to get off.

Everything you think or feel or do about this Tangle is generated from within its borders. That in turn keeps you inside those borders.

When we are stuck in a Tangle, the way we define or describe the problem is actually *part of the problem:* We might say, "My clutter rules my life," or "I have writer's block." We might say about a person, "He betrayed me." We might say about ourselves, "If I were thinner, people would love me." We might decide the solution is "I just have to try harder."

But in every case, those formulations don't help one little bit. They are all generated from inside the Tangle and they actually keep us stuck.

We can't think our way out of a Tangle. We are inside the cage of the problem because our thinking *itself* is part of the cage.

Let's just say that again. We can't conceptualize, or analyze, or problem-solve our way out—not if the problem is a Tangle. The very things that would work to solve even a complex problem—hard work, persistence, coming up with alternative solutions and trying them out—don't work with a Tangle.

Inside a Tangle, the best that all those efforts can accomplish is to keep things the same. Often they make things worse.

How we think about a Tangle, and what we think is causing it, is either not true or it is only a small, superficial part of what is really going on.

A Tangle defines what's real and what's possible

When we were growing up in the 1950s, it was simply unimaginable for us that a girl could grow up to be a president or a policeman or a jet pilot. That may seem hard to believe, but if we were asked what we wanted to be when we grew up, it was almost impossible to think of an answer that wasn't nurse or teacher or secretary. Any woman who went beyond these roles, like Amelia Earhart, was considered exceptional, extraordinary—and odd.

Part One: Untangling

Our point is that we felt limited, but we could not think beyond the boundary of that worldview. This same limiting structure applies with Tangles. From inside a Tangle, the world you live in and the nature of reality itself appears a certain way... and that seems "just the way it is."

When you are inside a Tangle, you can't see beyond the limited horizon of the Tangle. You can't even see that there is a limited horizon. Your thoughts about what kind of person you are or what you need to do to make things better are generated from inside the Tangle. Your beliefs about what is real and possible are restricted by the Tangle. Your feelings about the Tangle also originate from within the world of that Tangle.

A limited view of what is real and what is possible is inherent to Tangles.

In a Tangle there are always irreconcilable sides

People in Tangles are divided, at odds with themselves, and often at odds with the situations they're in as well. Struggle, both external and internal, is a characteristic of Tangles.

In Barbara's Tangle about her weight, she oscillated between two extremes: policing every mouthful or throwing caution to the winds and eating whatever (and however much) she wanted. She felt deprived and resentful when she was being "good" and disgusted and despairing when she let go of control.

In Ann's Tangle about writing, she spent a lot of time and energy trying to find ways to write easily. When she wasn't writing, she obsessed about writing. But, despite all that effort, not-writing kept on winning out. Giving up didn't work, and pushing harder didn't work either.

So inside a Tangle, there's no way forward. There seems to be inner turmoil no matter what we do. Nothing we do gets us where we want to go.

Tangles are emotional sinkholes

Tangles involve unwanted emotions and the struggle to manage and control them.

Usually we do not face our Tangles feeling calm and balanced. We are far more likely to be caught up in currents of emotion such as shame, sadness, anxiety, anger—or mired in the numbness that comes when powerful emotions are being locked up behind internal steel walls.

Tangled situations bring up emotions, and then those emotions bring challenges of their own. We may try to manage them, control them, handle them, or live authentically in spite of them.

For Barbara, her struggle over her weight brought up huge amounts of shame, self-disgust, and desperation. For Ann, her efforts to be a writer often came with feelings of helplessness, hopelessness, and inadequacy.

Additionally, in a Tangle you may fear you'll get overwhelmed or carried away by your emotions. You may feel intensely emotional and also afraid or embarrassed about being emotional. This adds another layer of complexity to the Tangle.

A Tangle always involves other people

There are always threads in a Tangle that connect to other people in some way. A Tangle might have to do with how you didn't get what you needed from others in the past. Or how you feel you need to hide or defend yourself from other people now. A Tangle might include beliefs about people, such as "I can't trust anybody" or "Relationships never work out." One way or another, other people are in your Tangle somewhere, even if how isn't obvious at first.

Barbara hated eating with other people. She wished she could enjoy sitting around the table having a meal with her friends. But she was always anxious that they would think she was eating too much or the wrong kinds of food. When she did eat with other people, she spent the whole time watching what they were eating and trying to match what they were doing. Eating with others became a kind of hell she avoided as much as possible.

Ann felt she needed her writing in order to receive acclaim and admiration—forms of love and approval—from other people. At the same time, showing her writing to others was fraught with danger. They might laugh at her, dismiss her, or be politely nice to her but not really get her point.

In a Tangle, other people are involved somehow—either you are entangled in outright conflict with them, or you protect yourself from them by limiting what you say and do.

In a Tangle you are isolated and alone

In a Tangle, you feel doomed to be alone with the problem the Tangle presents. You are afraid others would think less of you if they knew how

Part One: Untangling

you struggle with this, so you hide this whole area of your life from everyone around you. Being in a Tangle is like choosing to live with a hood over your head. You would rather others didn't see you clearly.

Barbara came to believe she had to deal with her problems herself. She had learned this from her father who said, "The McGavins don't tell people their business. We deal with things ourselves." When she was at university and struggling, it never occurred to her she could reach out and receive support. She felt that asking for help would be a shameful sign of her inherent deficiencies.

No one knew about Ann's struggles over her writing. Her friends saw a cheerful person who had hardly a care in the world. Her failure to be a writer was something that had to be hidden. She was sure she'd be laughed at for wanting to make a difference in the world by writing an important and helpful book.

A Tangle is full of self-blame and shame

Tangles are typically full of self-blame, self-doubt, of feeling like a fraud. "If people knew *this* about me, they wouldn't respect me..." or "...they would think I was weird..." or "...they would call me weak (lazy, a slob, childish...)." These "I'm not okay the way I am" feelings are an aspect of every Tangle we've ever encountered. In fact, one easy way to locate a Tangle is to ask yourself, "Where in my life do I feel I'm not good enough? Where do I fall short?" Or: "What do I feel I have to hide about myself?"

If you feel there is something wrong with you because you can't solve your Tangle, you are not alone. Among people we have worked with, Zuri felt bad about how she couldn't stop herself reaching for sugary snacks whenever she felt stressed or bored or upset about something. Jake felt ashamed about his longing for a physically attractive romantic partner when he should have been valuing other qualities more than how somebody looks. Noriko didn't like the way she felt grumpy and envious when she heard about someone else being happy. Alice didn't want anyone to know how lonely she felt and how much she hated being alone.

In addition to the shame about the Tangle itself, your persistent failure to change it is likely to bring more shame. Every time you try another diet, another job, another relationship, and these don't change anything either, another layer of self-disgust is added like sediment at the bottom of a stagnant pond.

The burden of shame and self-doubt is part of what makes a Tangle so hard to deal with. If nobody is allowed to know what you're going through, you're not able to get help from anyone. If seeing and admitting what's going on is too painfully shameful for something in you, you can't directly face the situation. So you are alone with your struggle and your shame.

Tangles make you want to give up, but you can't let go

If you've tried and tried, and always gotten the same stuck failure, you will probably believe that your Tangle can never change.

Barbara jokes that in her teens, by strictly following the Mayo Clinic Diet, she managed to reach her goal weight for about 20 seconds before she started gaining it all back again. By the time she was in her mid-thirties, she had tried every diet known to humanity—to no avail. She came to the point of feeling it was no use putting any more energy into this fruitless struggle, and yet she still held onto dreams of losing the weight that was dragging her down.

Over and over again, Ann gave up on writing a book that would transform people's lives. Once she got as far as writing a book proposal, but a single rejection was enough to cause her to trash the whole thing in despair. And yet she kept on dreaming of the day she would get a phone call from someone she'd never met, saying, "Thank you for writing that wonderful book."

You might feel like this too: fed up, despairing, dejected, and yet not able to let go. Although you feel there's no point trying anymore, you can't stop hoping that someday it will be different. And so you keep coming back to the Tangled issue. Something is important there. Something that won't let you go, like a little flicker of hope that refuses to die.

A Tangle touches on your very worth as a person

One of the strands of a Tangle is always about your worth as a person, your identity, who you feel you really are. When you can't figure out how to make things better, it may seem to you that your value as a person is compromised. Deep down, there is shame.

Every time Barbara looked in the mirror, she saw a fat, greedy, weak person who just couldn't control herself. Every time Ann looked in the mirror, she saw an insignificant person who was a miserable failure at doing something that mattered to help the world.

No matter how mundane it may appear on the surface, a Tangle always involves something more important: your sense of what kind of a person you are. This includes whether you are worthwhile or a good person, whether your needs matter and can be met, and whether you can live with autonomy and integrity.

When you are caught in a Tangle:

- You feel impossibly stuck.
- You are locked in an endless struggle with yourself and the world.
- There are lots of conflicting emotions involved, which can include fear, sadness, anger, shame, anxiety, frustration, despair, hope, longing.
- Every action you have tried or can imagine taking either simply doesn't work or, even worse, has negative consequences.
- Everything you think about the Tangle is part of the Tangle.
- Other people are involved somehow.
- It reduces your ability to live freely and fully in *all* areas of your life.

A Tangle involves:

- Your integrity and your autonomy.
- The nature of reality and what kind of a world you are living in.
- Your sense of worth as a human being, whether your needs matter and can be met, and ultimately your identity.

Even the most tangled up Tangle can Untangle

Barbara's painful relationship with food did shift. So did Ann's writer's block. So did Barbara's struggle with depression. So did Ann's problem with alcohol. And there were other Tangles we'll be telling you about later that also changed in fundamental ways.

We have said that Untangling can't happen when you're thinking inside the box. But Untangling requires more than just thinking outside the box. You will learn how to live outside the box.

More accurately, you *become* the new box—a bigger box that is larger than your Tangle. Let's put it another way: a Tangle transforms when you become bigger than the Tangle.

Untangling your Tangle will transform you—and your world—in ways you can't even begin to imagine. Old hurts heal. Old beliefs lose their grip. New possibilities appear. In a funny way, you could even say the Tangle itself is inviting you to live your fuller, truer life.

But you won't get there by thinking, analyzing, figuring out, pounding pillows, getting advice from friends, having more discipline or willpower, making resolutions, and certainly not by repeating what hasn't worked in the past. Something quite different needs to happen.

Part One: Untangling

Chapter 3
Tangled Up in Parts

ANN: I remember my shame and confusion on the day I realized I had a serious problem with alcohol. My thoughts were a jumble: "I can't trust myself any more. What am I going to do now?"

I was confronted with the facts: I'd been making bad choices. I'd been lying to myself. And the wonderful method that I had just traveled 6,000 miles to teach had not helped me shift this huge problem.

Not that my thoughts about it were that clear on that first day. Nothing at all was very clear... except that I didn't want to drink anymore. But I didn't know how long I could hold out before I reached for the bottle again.

When Barbara offered to help and suggested, "Maybe you need to have a relationship with the Part of you that wants to drink," I felt an inner "Yes." Even hearing the phrase "the Part of you that wants to drink" was helpful somehow.

Fortunately, we had time right then and there. We sat across from each other, using the Focusing partnership format we taught in our workshops.

I closed my eyes and brought my awareness into my body, especially my throat, chest, and stomach area. I said out loud, "I am curious about the Part of me that wants to drink and I want to get to know it better."

Soon I could feel that Part of me inside my chest. It was like a strong, hungry, caged bear pulling at its chains, trying to get loose. I said to it inwardly, "Hello, I know you are there." I sensed it felt angry at being caged and I let it know I could see how angry it was.

And so my inner relationship with this Part of me began.

Part One: Untangling

BARBARA: When Ann told me about her drinking and how helpless she felt, I thought about some inner work I had done just a few months before.

For most of my life I had carried a persistent sense at the core of my being that I could not and never would be okay. Dying seemed the only hope of escape from something that felt unbearable and like it would continue forever. The big shift came when I started to see it was a *Part of me,* not all of me, that wanted to die. Although the painful feelings were still there, I was more than those feelings. I could *be with* the Part of me that felt like that. I didn't have to be taken over by it, and if I wasn't taken over by it, I could pay a different kind of attention to it. Over time I formed a compassionate and accepting inner relationship with it.

What it needed from me became clear: to be sensed just exactly the way it was—just as painful and despairing as it felt. I also needed to be able to say to this Part of me that it could be the way it was for as long as it needed to be, that I would not try to change it. I was here *for* it.

It was why I knew that a relationship with the Part that wanted to drink could hold the key for Ann. And there were sure to be other Parts that needed her attention as well.

Why talk about Parts?

When we started relating to aspects of our experience as Parts, the Tangles we faced became much easier to explore. If it was a Part of Ann that wanted to drink, then Ann could relate to that part of her with compassion, be curious about it, and get to know it better. If it was a Part of Barbara that wanted to die, then she could treat that Part of her with acceptance and love, knowing she was more than that Part. Moving into relationship with Parts of ourselves was what made it possible for our Tangles to shift, release, and transform.

Some people are bothered by this talk about Parts. They say, "I want to be more whole, not more in bits." But truthfully, being "in bits" is a common experience. You know how sometimes you are of two minds about something, how sometimes you have more than one feeling, or sometimes you do something you wish you didn't and then tell yourself off for having done it?

The truth about you is that you are a whole person even when it feels like you are in pieces. Then why talk about Parts? Quite simply, we do it because it helps. Using Parts language and Parts concepts enables us to form relationships with troubling or puzzling aspects of our reactions, our behavior, and our feelings. And it is in having empathic relationships with these aspects of our lives that Untangling can take place.

Tangled up in Parts

In Tangles, Parts can seem like different people inside of you. They have different points of view, often seeing the world in radically different ways. They hold different beliefs about what is right or good or healthy or how you should live. They have different desires, different fears, different dreams for you. Some of them tell you what they think of you or what they think you should be doing. Some of them don't talk much, they just do things or refuse to do things.

All of these Parts have different concerns. They are afraid of different things. They develop different strategies to deal with the situations you are in. Maybe Part of you shies away from going further with something you want to do while another Part of you is berating you for being a wimp. Perhaps you want to reveal what is deep in your heart, but Part of you draws back and in, making you smaller, more defended, less alive.

And Parts don't just have different points of view. All of them have *limited* points of view. None of them can see the full picture. They cannot have a sense of the whole Tangle, let alone a sense of something bigger than the Tangle. Because Parts only have limited points of view, they can only deal with the little bit of the Tangle they are aware of. Any solutions they utilize are incomplete and inadequate.

Parts often pull you in different directions, either by openly battling or quietly undermining each other. One side may have a loud voice, and the other is silent yet has a powerful impact on your life. One Part in your Tangle may be on top for a while, and then it flips and the other one gets the upper hand. They push and pull, back and forth, round and round in their anxiety, fear, and desire... and with each fraught transfer of power, you probably feel increasingly frustrated, helpless, mired, disgusted with yourself. You may wind up feeling like a failure because no matter what you do, you can't resolve the struggle. Being caught in a tussle between Parts in a Tangle is no fun.

Part One: Untangling

"It feels like me"

When you are living inside a Tangle, "Who I am" becomes slippery. Am I the one who drank the whole bottle of wine and skipped dinner? Or am I the one who is disgusted at having done so and determined to get this under control? They both feel like me.

When you see the world through the eyes of a Part of you, when your actions are based on its beliefs and fueled by its emotions, we call that being "merged" with a Part—or being "identified" with it. What you say, do, think, and believe when you are merged with a Part are actually the thoughts, actions, and beliefs of that Part. The result: who you are and what you believe varies widely depending on which Part you're merged with. No wonder having a Tangle is confusing.

It's crucial to be able to recognize when you are merged with a Part in your Tangle, and doing so can be distinctly challenging. We will be spending a lot of time looking at how to recognize the many different ways you can be merged with your Parts—and how you can unmerge from them.

Where do Parts come from?

When something difficult happens, your body has a feeling of the forward momentum of life being stopped. That, in itself, is at least uncomfortable. You also have an emotional reaction to being prevented from going forward. You might feel frustrated or bewildered or upset or sad or angry or scared about it. These emotional reactions are a natural part of your body's response to not being able to get your life moving again in the way that would be right for you.

Your Tangle originally formed because you experienced something painfully difficult that proved impossible for you to work through. In trying to deal with it, you were confronted with a "damned if I do, damned if I don't" dilemma. Dealing with it would have meant having to put yourself in a situation that felt life-threatening.

There are many kinds of danger you might have faced, but the danger that creates Tangles threatens your connections with the people who are essential in your life. In a Tangle those important people around you, instead of helping, were actually part of what made the situation impossible to resolve.

Ann's father was emotionally distant and sometimes sarcastic. Compared to what many other kids suffer, that might not seem so bad. Yet Ann's most tangled Tangles led back to all the times she reached to her father for love and approval, and over and over he turned away. It became impossible for Ann to directly seek love and approval from her father. Later in her life this affected all her close relationships with men.

In Barbara's family expressing any kind of "negative" emotion was quickly squelched. She vividly remembers her father saying, "The McGavins don't feel nervous." She came to feel the only safe thing to do with all her emotions was to hide them.

Most of the people who have done Untangling with us have had painful experiences with their parents or siblings, teachers, schoolmates, people in some kind of position of power over them. When they were exuberant, they were mocked. When they shared something they had made, they were ignored. When their boundaries were disrespected, it wasn't safe to speak up. They have been criticized, belittled, controlled, dismissed, betrayed. Some have been physically attacked. They were not safe to be themselves, freely and openly. They were not safe to express their needs for support, understanding, help or love.

When you can't resolve the tough, confusing situation you're facing, and the feelings about your life being blocked cannot be felt, those feelings become frozen. When feelings are frozen, they cannot shift and evolve. In that impossible situation, you could not live freely in any of the ways that would have been right for you. What should have been a straightforward, if painful, experience has now become stuck—stopped. We call this a Stoppage—and from a Stoppage, Parts develop.

So what are Parts trying to do?

Parts develop around a Stoppage to try to protect you from experiencing the unbearableness of it even as they are also trying to go beyond it. Parts are attempts to solve the problem of the Stoppage, but, as we have already said, Parts are limited, so their solutions are limited too.

When we can't get everything we need, Parts try to get us some of what we need. When the feelings that get stirred up are too much to experience, Parts try to keep us shut down or distracted or feeling something else instead.

Part One: Untangling

When we can't go forward as *all* of who we are, Parts are an attempt to go forward with *part* of who we are.

Parts come into being for three fundamental reasons: so you can get at least some of what you needed; so you don't have to feel the full pain of what happened; and so the incomplete and not entirely adequate solutions and strategies of other Parts will not make things even worse for you.

Every time Barbara expressed how she was feeling, her father would let her know that kind of behavior was simply not acceptable. Over time, a Part of her came to believe that showing her feelings meant she was flawed and inherently unloveable. In order to protect herself, she learned to hide her feelings by any means possible. She developed a Part that worked endlessly to present a stoical, ultra-private facade, no matter what she actually felt, to manage her feelings of being fundamentally worthless. She became so practiced at donning her mask of invisibility that when other people would look at her, it was as if Barbara had vanished.

There was another side to this as well. As Barbara grew older and moved out into the world, she started to feel the limitations of hiding who she was all the time. She wanted to be more free, more authentic and genuine, but she didn't know how, so she would blurt out intimate details about her life to people she barely knew and then feel devastated and disgusted with herself when they recoiled from her.

This is an example of how Parts take on tough jobs, help us survive, help us to stay safe. But because they are "partial," they don't have the resources of our full selves, and the solutions they come up with will always be incomplete. When those attempts fail to solve the problem, other Parts with different strategies try to fix the holes and gaps that have been created. But, of course, these further attempts to fix things are also incomplete, and the result is a tangled mess of different strategies, competing and arguing with each other.

And this is why, when we talk about Tangles, we need to talk about Parts.

How your Parts need you to be with them

When you recognize you have been identified with a Part, that gives you the opportunity to disidentify (unmerge) from it. As you disidentify from it, you can feel you are more than just that one Part of you.

When you become grounded in that larger sense of yourself, you have more options and more freedom than a Part does. You can see a wider perspective that is not limited by a Part's point of view.

That's what happened when Ann recognized it was a Part of her, not all of her, that wanted to drink. It's what happened when Barbara recognized it was a Part of her, not all of her, that wanted to die.

Recognizing something in you is a Part raises the question of how you treat your Parts. There may be an intense temptation to squash troublesome Parts, cut them out, get rid of them. "If that's what's been causing the problem, I'll just eliminate it and we'll be fine."

There are actually two huge problems with that approach. One, you are becoming identified with another Part that has an opinion about something in you and that simply doesn't work. Two—and this is even more important than problem number one—if you managed to get rid of a Part of you, you'd be eliminating something valuable and precious from who you are.

Every one of your Parts is a custodian of essential aspects of who you are, aspects you haven't been able to live openly and freely. To be able to live fully, you'll need those attributes, qualities, and energy. When you are able to be with your Parts in the ways they need from you, those abilities become freely available in all areas of your life in ways that fit with your life as it now is.

Parts need now what was missing when your Tangle first formed: understanding, compassion, and empathy. In other words, they need your love.

PART TWO

ALL TANGLED UP

All human situations are much more intricate than our concepts and phrases can capture.
    Eugene Gendlin, *Focusing-Oriented Psychotherapy*, p. 58

When your Tangle shifts, everything shifts. Living is an intricate process, and when life flows, it can flow in unexpected and unplanned ways. We can't know in advance precisely what "being Untangled" will be like. It's never exactly what we thought it would be.

Living a life without even thinking about alcohol is like living in a different country and speaking a completely different language. Living a life without feeling inadequate all the time changes everything. When your Tangle untangles, a whole previously unimaginable world of possibilities becomes available.

You're probably eager to get on with the adventure of exploring your Untangled life. And we will be showing you how to get there. But first you need to get curious about what is utterly impossible in your life.

In this next section of the book, *All Tangled Up*, you will meet six patterns of impossibility that occur in Tangles. For each kind of pattern, we'll describe the kind of thing that happens, show you how to identify the Parts typically involved, and point to how they can begin to untangle.

In every one of these types of Tangles there are Parts. We'll be talking about how to identify them, and we'll see how tricky it can be not to merge with them or to try to fix, manipulate, or control them. We'll show how easy it can be to continue the patterns of behavior and thought that have been keeping you stuck.

In fact, it's possible that your Parts will show up as you are reading these chapters, bringing feelings of worry, shame, or hopelessness about your own life, or reactions of rebellion and defiance. This is natural. All the feelings and reactions that arise as you read are understandable.

Read gently. Be aware, notice and acknowledge what you feel. Take breaks when you need to. There's no need to charge ahead at full speed. You can trust your own inner sense of rightness for when to take a rest and when to go on.

We hope you will recognize your own struggles with what feels impossibly Tangled. It's quite likely that your Tangles will have elements of some or even all of these patterns, but even if you don't recognize your own Tangle here at all, you'll still get important clues about how to approach your Tangle so its knots can loosen.

And do keep going. There is life beyond Tangles.

Part Two: All Tangled Up

40

Chapter 4
*H*IJACK

ANN: On a typical day in the early 1990s I would wake up in the morning feeling a bit hungover. The night before, I'd started—and finished—a bottle of Chardonnay, followed with a brandy or two. And because I didn't feel proud of that, I'd decide that today I wouldn't drink.

"Of course I don't really have a drinking problem. I get up and get my work done every day! So it'll be easy not to drink. And today I just won't." A clear, unequivocal decision. Easy to make. Easy to do. All I had to do was not drink. Right?

Then as it got closer and closer to the evening and time to stop working, whispers would start. "I deserve to give myself pleasure," they would say. "I work really hard! I need to relax."

Countering these whispers, other voices arose. "Getting drunk every night is not a very enlightened thing to do," they said. "You're a respected Focusing teacher. People look to you for leadership. What would people think if they knew how much you drank?" But there was a counter to that, too. "Other people drink a lot more than I do!"

Back and forth. As the day went on, the argument became more and more heated, and occupied more and more of my mental space.

Then at 5 PM, with no decision of any kind having been made, I found myself in the nearest liquor store, buying a bottle of wine. The argument was over. There was total inner peace. Without "me" deciding to, I was all set to spend another evening getting drunk.

What happened? How did I get from "today I won't drink" to pouring myself another glass of my favorite Chardonnay?

By the end of 1994, Barbara and I had begun to have a "Parts" understanding of how I had been using alcohol. We started to say it was "something in me" that wanted to drink. This Part had its own reasons for drinking that weren't what we assumed. In fact, they completely surprised us.

From a Parts perspective, what happened was that, come 5 o'clock, the Part that wanted to drink took over. It was as if someone stole the car keys and went joyriding. We recognized that this kind of complete seizing-of-control by a Part is a pattern that occurs in many Tangles. We call it *Hijack*.

When a Part of you has climbed into the driver's seat, you might feel as if you no longer have a choice about what you are doing. We're not saying you don't have choice. But when you get hijacked, exercising a choice becomes very difficult.

Hijacks are, in fact, ubiquitous in Tangles. We've never known a Tangle that doesn't include a Part doing something in a way that feels dangerously out of control to something else in you.

"I wish I would stop doing that!"

"I really shouldn't be doing that... but I can't stop myself" is the kind of thing people say when they have this kind of Tangle. You may feel nearly powerless against what could be called "self-indulgence" or "lack of willpower" or "being out of control."

Anything you find yourself doing repetitively, feeling you really should stop but you can't, would be a Tangle of this type. For example: playing computer games endlessly, or racking up too many online purchases, or staying up way past the time you wanted to be in bed. It might be something that you don't even find enjoyable, yet still you find yourself doing it. Such as checking your email for the umpteenth time. "What a waste of time!" you moan later... but then find yourself mindlessly doing it again.

If it happens over and over, and you feel helpless to stop it even though you've tried everything you can think of—it's probably a Tangle.

What's it like when a Part hijacks you?

BARBARA: While writing this chapter I was hijacked at least four times.

They were relatively benign Hijacks, as Hijacks go, but they were still Hijacks. They were actions taken by a Part of me to help me avoid experiencing the discomfort and frustration I was feeling while trying to write this chapter. This Part felt that hijacking me was its only option for getting me away from those uncomfortable, unwanted feelings.

Let's look at how that played out. First, tension began to build up in my body. As I struggled to find the right words for what I was trying to say, I didn't turn my attention toward the feelings in my body. I just kept on struggling. The tension continued to build until suddenly I found myself opening my iPad and watching the next gripping episode of *Waking the Dead*. While I was watching, I felt no tension. I was absorbed in the story. Just as with Ann in the liquor store, peace reigned.

After the episode finished, I became aware of how annoyed something in me was that I had "wasted all that time." It was almost shouting at me, "You keep doing this and you're never going to finish this damn book!"

I went back to writing, and after a while the same process repeated. Rising tension, followed by being hijacked into an absorbing activity, followed by a backlash of shaming by an extremely anxious and frustrated Part.

What's happening when you get hijacked?

Often Hijacks happen without you being aware of them. You look at the empty cigarette pack and think, "I don't remember smoking all those cigarettes!" Or you are shocked at the total on your credit card statement: "Did I really spend all that money?" Or you look at the clock and realize you've just spent the last three hours watching random videos.

If you were able to pause and notice your feelings before the Hijack happened, you would notice discomfort and a dilemma. You might be almost unaware of those feelings except as something familiar in the background. They are often hidden except as the most fleeting of sensations before you get hijacked.

In a Hijack, there is some kind of inner dilemma about what to do. Do I stop work and take care of myself or keep going for another hour? Do I grab a bag of chips and turn on the TV or do I put on my shoes and go for a walk? Do I speak up about an issue that matters to me or do I grab a chocolate bar and surf the internet? Do I keep on pushing to try to find the right words or do I stop and pay attention to how it feels to be struggling? For some reason, the best next step—what you would need to do so this situation can really move forward—is blocked.

Why do you get hijacked?

At first glance it may seem obvious what a hijacking Part is trying to do. On the face of it, it's trying to get you to drink or buy stuff or eat yourself into oblivion. But is that what it's really trying to do for you? What's behind that surface goal?

You won't really know the motives driving a hijacking Part until you form an empathic relationship with it and get to know how it itself feels. This much we know: every Part has some good reason for doing what it's doing—from its point of view.

A Hijack is not just a bad habit. Yes, there are bad habits and there are ways of extinguishing those habits. A Hijack is driven by something deeper than that. You experience your Hijack as a frustrating problem, but, in fact, it is an attempt by your Parts to help you.

All kinds of painful and difficult feelings come up in a Tangle, including frustration, shame, and even despair about failing to resolve it. You have Parts that want to help you avoid those feelings by distracting you, anesthetizing you, or giving you something more "fun" to do.

Hijacking Parts can be trying to soothe or numb your feelings. That is perhaps the most common kind of Hijack driving many behaviors that could be called addictive. This includes using alcohol or food or other substances and behaviors such as persistently staying up late or bingeing on Netflix. Any of these behaviors can be the result of Parts hijacking you so you don't have to feel something they are afraid would be too painful to endure.

Those same Parts might be trying to give you resources for surviving what life is throwing at you, but in a way that is deniable. Ann remembers that when she was working too hard, getting drunk in the evening was a way to relax quickly without having to admit she needed to relax.

Ann's drinking Part used alcohol to jump over the boundary of her daily life to access playful, sensuous and creative aspects of who she is. But something in her found it too scary to live permanently in that freer way. It felt safer being able to wake up the next morning back inside the fence of her workaday world.

Pseudo relief

Barbara remembers what a relief it was to stop trying to control her eating as she picked up the chocolate or chicken or that extra bit of potato sitting on the plate in front of her. Ann says she felt relief as soon as she stepped into the liquor store—long before she actually had the first sip.

In that moment, all the dissenting Parts fell silent, as if they had been drugged, bound and thrown into a cupboard. *During* the Hijack they were nowhere to be found.

This kind of relief is *not* a good indicator of a Tangle being resolved. It is the relief that arises from the temporary cessation of the struggle between Parts. Inside a Tangle, it is all the relief we can ever know.

Backlash

Perhaps the most painful part of a Hijack comes after it's over. After the tranquilizing effects of the chocolate or the booze or the super-late-night gaming binge have worn off, you may become identified with a shaming Part, disgusted by your behavior, telling you to never do that again. Or you may become identified with a shamed Part and feel mortified about your behaviors or your feelings.

Unfortunately, this only adds to the burden the Part that hijacked you feels. Now it has not only the original feelings it was trying to help you avoid, it also has feelings of shame about what it did to try to deal with them. All of this makes it more likely you will be hijacked again in the future.

Parts in a struggle

As you get to know the Parts involved in a Hijack, you will probably discover that they have relationships among themselves. It is likely you will encounter a very low-trust, high-conflict relationship between a hijacking Part and at least one other Part that is determined to stop it.

Being hijacked is becoming merged with the Part that's eating or shopping or drinking. In reaction to that, it's easy to become merged with the Part

Part Two: All Tangled Up

that feels powerless and frustrated when you are being hijacked, as our student Courtney realized. "I'm spending hours looking at the sales on the internet when I don't want to, and I'm buying all sorts of stuff I don't need," she told us. "There is a Part of me that really wants to do things differently, but it's not strong enough. The shopping Parts are succeeding in dominating my life."

You can tell from the language she is using—"not strong enough" and "dominating my life"—that she is identified with the point of view of the Part that is upset about her having been hijacked.

Just as there are Parts trying to oppose a hijacking Part in your Tangle, there are probably also Parts in your Tangle that actively assist the hijacking one. They say things like, "You can start that diet tomorrow" or "You deserve to enjoy yourself."

Parts that oppose and Parts that assist may argue with each other—a lot! A Part that's supporting it finds reasons that it is okay for the hijacking Part to do what it wants. A Part that's opposing the Hijack calls those reasons "excuses" and evidence of "having no willpower."

What allows Parts in a Hijack to transform?

After you recognize that a Hijack has happened, the next step is to not shame yourself for it. That doesn't help. You just feel worse about yourself and your life. Instead, you might start from the assumption that all your Parts are trying to help you—somehow.

Acknowledging the positive intent behind a Hijack can help keep you from becoming identified with any of the Parts involved: the hijacking Part, the shaming Part, or the assisting Part.

The war over Hijack is endless... until *you*, not identified with any Part, arrive. Inside the Tangle, you might have felt your only choice was to either let your hijacking Parts run wild or to be strict, controlling, and repressive with them. But that's another Part of you that feels like it has to choose between one of those alternatives.

The way to Untangle is not by agreeing with either one of these sides. Rather, you'll establish a relationship of curiosity and empathy with the hijacking Part in which you neither shame it nor indulge it. You will also come to understand the points of view of the Parts that are reacting to it.

As we've said, the hijacking Part has its reasons for behaving as it does. When you are neither identified with it, nor identified with the Part of you that wants to control it, you'll be able to listen compassionately to what it's been trying to do for you. In Chapter Thirteen, *The Magic of Empathy,* we'll show you how to create and nurture the compassionate inner relationship a hijacking Part needs. In that inner relationship, the ability to take action and make choices will shift back to you, your larger Self. The other Parts, the ones that have been trying to control or enable the hijacking one, will also relax, their vigilance no longer needed.

BARBARA: As I grapple with writing this chapter, I am spending time with a Part of me that wants to eat. And right now, I'm *not* hijacked by the Part that wants to eat. I'm aware of it. I can sense it in my body as a kind of restless ache in my stomach area. I am here with it.

And I'm also aware of an anxious, frustrated Part that has opinions about the Part that wants to eat. I feel like it's dancing on my right shoulder. It says, "This eating thing is ruining your life!" I can sense how easy it could be to join this Part: make the hijacking Part the problem, try to control it by calling it names and setting up strict rules about food and eating.

If I'm identified with the Part that says, "It's ruining my life," then nothing new can happen. Whether the Part that wants to eat *is* "ruining" my life or not is actually irrelevant right now. If I get upset about the thought that my life is being ruined by the Part that eats, I'm identified with the Part that is feeling upset, and I'm still inside the Tangle.

What I need first and foremost is to be able to bring compassionate, curious awareness to each of these Parts, instead of being identified with a controlling Part or a rebellious Part or a suffering Part. I can dis-identify (unmerge) from the Part that's feeling anxious and turn back to the Part that wants to eat. I can give it company without trying to change it in any way. I can simply get how it is from *its* point of view.

I'm aware of Parts that are worried about my potential "loss of control." I can sense how they are poised to start calling me "greedy" or "weak," to try to get me back in line. I sense other Parts ready to react with shame and embarrassment to those criticisms. I can also feel a rebellious Part saying, "Hey! I deserve some pleasure!" and "Don't you dare take away my freedom!"

So I pause and take some time to acknowledge all of these Parts and then noticing what Part of me is needing my company right now. This lets me develop a deeper empathic relationship with *all* of these Parts.

It's a different world

Ann no longer has a Part that wants to drink. Not drinking alcohol is easy for her whatever the circumstances. She doesn't miss it—at all. In fact, she's a big fan of sparkling water. (She says the bubbles give her that little thrill.)

Getting from where she was in 1994 to where she is now has been a process. It started with acknowledging there was a Part that wanted to drink and another Part that was anxious about that Part's behavior.

This may sound like a small step, but it's actually huge. To move from "It's disgusting to drink so much" to "Something in me wants to drink, *and* another something in me is anxious and worried about that behavior" is as big as the difference between night and day.

Recognizing and unmerging from those two Parts made something possible that hadn't been possible before: an empathic inner relationship with each one of them. The Part that wanted to drink revealed how it had been trying to protect Ann from confusing, conflicted feelings about her father after his death. And the anxious, worried Part was able to get in touch with the freedom and confidence that it really wanted for Ann. In Chapter Thirteen, *The Magic of Empathy,* we'll tell you more about how this process works and how it leads to transformation.

Not drinking at all was only one possible outcome of Ann's issue with alcohol becoming Untangled. A different outcome might have been feeling comfortable and at ease having a glass of wine with dinner. But either way, she wouldn't find herself in the liquor store grabbing the Chardonnay and getting drunk instead of having her dinner. Barbara still eats chocolate—every day. But it isn't a whole bar, wolfed down in secret. When something in her wants to eat when she isn't hungry, Barbara knows it's not because she is weak or greedy. Something in her needs her loving attention.

Chapter 5
Takeover

BARBARA: When my daughter was born, I wanted to be the best mother possible. I wanted to be loving, caring, and supportive—and not make any of the mistakes my parents had made. If you have children, you are probably already laughing out loud.

Of course I failed to live up to these ideals over and over again. They were ideals formed out of my own experiences of pain and struggle as a child. But although I had a sense of what was wrong, I didn't know what would be right.

I felt in over my head almost all the time. I didn't have a clue how to be a good mum. I didn't know what to do with all the feelings that came up when my little daughter couldn't be soothed to sleep or had a several-hours-long tantrum or refused to eat what I'd put in front of her.

I was exhausted and insecure and felt utterly alone a lot of the time. I was thousands of miles away from my own mother, and I wasn't sure I actually trusted her advice anyway. I didn't have many friends I could reach out to to either, so I turned to all the latest books and magazines on parenting. That seemed eminently reasonable to me, because you can learn so much from the distilled experience and wisdom found in books.

However, as I tried diligently to follow all those instructions, something happened: I became more and more rigid and anxious. I constantly compared my parenting to the "good parenting" in the books. I was more often focused on doing it "right" than on loving my daughter.

What do you do when you don't know what to do? It makes a lot of sense to look for someone to give you advice, help, and guidance. If someone encourages and supports you to grow and mature in your own competence and confidence, that can make all the difference.

Part Two: All Tangled Up

But say you are faced with a situation that's more than you can cope with on your own, and there's no one there to help you. Or the person you turn to is too busy, or unsupported themselves. They might be well-meaning but not have the skills you need. Or perhaps, instead of being caring and capable, the person you have to rely on is unreliable, controlling, dismissive, undermining, or even dangerous.

In the absence of anyone who can help you know what would be right to do, Parts step in to try to fill that gap.

"Okay. Do this!"

In a Tangle, if you are feeling lost and unsure, at least one Part will rush in to try to rescue you. It's as if it is saying, "Well, somebody's got to take care of you. I'm here!" It is trying to take on the job of being the grownup. Unfortunately, it *isn't* grown up. It's a Part.

Parts like this formed when you were much younger. They think and feel and see the world in much the same way as when they first formed—so they aren't grown up. They are like children trying to take on adult responsibilities, with all the limitations and stress that come with being so young.

One of the most common signs that a Part is trying to take charge is how rigid your thinking becomes. You have categorical, black-and-white opinions about what you are like, what other people are like, and what the world is like. There is only one right thing to believe. Only one right choice you can make. Only one right way to do anything. Right or wrong. Good or bad. No exceptions. No excuses.

When you are identified with an anxious Part like this, you may feel that total control is necessary: "I have to track *every* lick and bite, and if I don't I've blown it completely!" You feel you have no choice: "I have to make sure *everyone* is happy *all the time* or I'm a selfish, uncaring person," "I *must* win or I will be a total failure."

Whatever it is about, and however it is expressed, the drive to control your thoughts, your emotions and your actions becomes paramount. We call this a *Takeover*.

These Parts can have all sorts of ideas about how to try to support you. They read books, they ask friends, they go to workshops. They give you advice. They find inspiring quotes. It may all make sense, and the ideas might even be good ones, but inside a Tangle this doesn't help. This is tinkering with superficial details when what is needed is a much deeper transformation.

"You're going to fail!"

When an anxious Part becomes even more frantic, it starts to try and control you by going on the attack. It makes dark and dreadful predictions about your future: "You're going to fail" or "You're going to die alone." In its attempts to control behavior like drinking or eating too much, it says, "You're going to ruin your health" or "You'll get so fat you won't even be able to move."

These categorical Predictions of Doom (as we call them) come from a Part panicking that you're heading for an awful future. It is acutely worried that it won't be able to do anything to stop you.

A Part may use disaster movies of car crashes or images of homeless camps to try to control you: "See? This is what's going to happen to you!" The whole point is to try to persuade you—actually another Part of you—to follow the narrow path that this Part is sure will save you.

"Don't tell me what to do!"

In Takeover situations, Parts rouse each other. The more anxious and controlling the "Do this!" Part is, the more another Part will rebel against it. Parts trying to wield control can be cunning about putting pressure on other Parts to do something. But Parts can sense when they are being strong-armed to do something even when that pressure isn't obvious.

> **BARBARA:** I have been with WeightWatchers since 2012. I reached my goal weight in 2018 and have been maintaining it since then. This has given me many opportunities to notice the difference between when a controlling Part tries to run the show, when a Part hijacks my eating, and when I make my own free choices.
>
> When I am tired or something in me is stressed or upset, I have a Part that still tries to help soothe me by eating. I know how it feels in my body when it wants me to relax and reach for "comfort food."
>
> This, of course, frightens a Part that doesn't trust I will not simply succumb to being hijacked, eating anything I can get my hands on.

I can sense how these Parts can get locked into a tug-of-war over my eating.

Once I become aware these two Parts are stuck together in a standoff, I can acknowledge them both. Their grip on me lessens as each one trusts that I am here now and I will not be taken over by either one.

Collaboration

During a Takeover, although we might see Parts feeling resentful and refusing to act, we might also see them collaborating. When Parts collaborate, they share a world view. They agree on the problem and the solution. A Part takes on the responsibility for deciding what you should do and sets the agenda. Other Parts, able to act, then carry it out.

An insecure Part might welcome another Part's certainty. A Part that doesn't know what to do might embrace a friendly, seemingly confident Part with open arms. When a Part that is able to act collaborates willingly with a Part that is trying to manage it, it tries its best to fulfill the commands it's being given.

Barbara striving to be a perfect mother is a good example of this. There were at least two Parts involved: one Part feeling insecure and alone in her parenting and another Part trying to help her by providing information so she would know what she should do.

Collaborations between Parts may even be an effective stopgap way of dealing with what they consider to be the problem. When Parts work together, there is often a feeling of satisfaction, pleasure, and pride. There might be a sense of "Look at me! See how well I'm doing!" underlying the action. These collaborations can feel good, at least for a while.

The problem is, it's still a Tangle. Parts, with narrow views and limited resources, are still in charge, and any equilibrium that is reached will be uneasy and temporary.

As a Part that can act tries to fulfill the ideals of a controlling Part, its actions can become driven. Workaholism and perfectionism are examples of this. The urgent, anxiety-laced quality of these kinds of actions is a way you can tell they are the actions a Part of you is taking.

: All Tangled Up

...trying to take control of your thinking and direct your actions. ...ay be a Part rebelling against being controlled or a Part may be ...collaborating with a controlling Part. In Chapter Twelve, *Always ...r One More,* we'll show you how to recognize more than one Part in ...ngle, and in Chapter Thirteen, *The Magic of Empathy,* you'll learn ...enable each Part to feel fully heard and understood.

...listen carefully to a Part trying to exert control, it can start to trust ...e there, taking charge of your life yourself. Then it can begin to let ...s need to be in charge.

...listen carefully to a Part rebelling against being controlled, you ...p it to express its underlying determination to stand up for your ...ticity and autonomy.

...the case of a Part that has been trying to live up to the ideals of a ...ling Part, you can start to acknowledge the underlying feelings of ...ity that drive it to seek certainty outside of itself.

...sense how hard all these Parts have been striving to help you and ...u from a terrible fate, you can let them know how much you appreciate all they have done for you. Deep empathy will help them to feel ...cared for, and loved. The ultimate result: the Parts that have been ...to control you relax and trust you to make your own life choices.

A Part that can act often feels guilty and asham[ed]... to control has taken over. No matter how hard it [tries, it is not able] to fully satisfy the demands of the Part controll[ing it...] always shifting, always that little bit out of reac[h.]

A Part striving to reach the unattainable goal set b[y ...] become unbalanced and break down. Some extre[me examples are] the workaholic who plummets into a nervous bre[akdown, ...] who starts to binge and purge, or the "A" student [who] fails to maintain his grade average.

Don't we need someone to tell us [what is right] and wrong?

Your protective Parts believe they are what keep [...] onto and enforce rules because they don't trust y[ou to act appro]priately without them. It is true that many of the ru[les that allow] people to live together in community are given b[y ... and you] needed to learn them as part of growing up. But tha[t is not like having] an angel sitting on your shoulder, telling you what [to do.] The truth is, *you* can develop your ability to respo[nd to the] situations in your life. You don't need your Parts t[o ... You can] develop your ability to be bigger than your Tangl[e and respond in a way that fits] what fits the situations you live in. You know fro[m ... that] it isn't right to hurt or take advantage of others. Y[ou can act in a] compassionate and caring way without being con[trolled] by your Parts.

So our answer is no. When you are living beyond [your Parts, you don't] need your Parts to tell you what is right and wrong. [When you live beyond your Parts in your] life, you are more free to live in ways that meet the [needs of the] situation without having to follow arbitrary rules an[d ...]

What allows Parts in a Takeover to tr[ust?]

To unmerge from the Parts in a Takeover, you nee[d to recognize what you] have become merged with something in you. Ther[e may be more than] one Part involved, so you will need to recognize [each of the] various Parts tangled up together. In a Takeover [the Part ...]

Chapter 6
Rebellion

BARBARA: When I was newly pregnant with my daughter and freshly out of work, I spent many hours holed up under my warm and comforting blankets thinking about what I would do when I got up. My do-today list included simple things like doing the laundry and going out and buying food and then cooking it.

I would work it all out in minute detail—and then go back to sleep for another hour or two. Then it would be too late to do any of that today. I would tell myself, "I'll do it tomorrow." Tomorrow would dawn, and I would cling to my blankets, feeling tired and overwhelmed, and like the last thing I wanted to do was get up and tackle my have-to-do list.

It reminded me of an earlier time, at university, when stresses were piling up, and it dawned on me that if I didn't go to class, no one in this large university would actually notice. So instead of going to class, I slept. That way I could push the whole world away.

In later years, before Ann and I started to develop Untangling, my tendency to hide out would return periodically. As soon as I started to feel under stress, I would retreat to my bed. Instead of going out and having fun on the weekends, I would shut out the world by curling up all day with another novel or sleeping my life away. No matter how much I tried to force myself to get my act together, I spent a lot of time under my duvet.

You just don't do it

Your apartment is a mess. Your desk would thrill an archaeologist—there seem to be layers going back to prehistoric times. You've got a to-do list that just keeps getting longer. Your closets are full of clothes you haven't worn since high school, but you never get around to taking them to the charity

Part Two: All Tangled Up

shop. You want to write, or play the piano, or get your website up, or finish your degree, or make a difference in the world... but it doesn't happen.

This kind of Tangle is the territory of broken promises—to others, of course, but even more importantly, to yourself. It feels like you've failed yourself over and over again. As the weeks and months go by, all the self-recrimination builds up, and you start believing you are an irredeemable hot mess of a human being. You are dogged by a draggy sense of carrying around the burden of all the stuff that is still unfinished.

Repeatedly you resolve to do better, saying, "Tomorrow I will start the plan. Tomorrow I will write the outline. Tomorrow I will make that call..."

But if it's a Tangle, when tomorrow comes you still don't do it.

On strike

If even a bit of this sounds familiar, you probably have a kind of Tangle that we call an action block. Parts that refuse to act are like strikers who walk out and bring everything to a grinding halt. It's as if a Part of you is damned if it is going to do whatever it is supposed to be doing. If it could talk, it would say, "I'm not doing that! No way. You can't make me."

An action block is also a kind of Hijack. The Hijack is carried out by the Part that doesn't do it.

It doesn't write. It crawls under the covers and refuses to do anything but sleep. It doesn't organize the taxes, or go to the gym, or clean out the closet. It's the one that doesn't go into the studio and record your new song, and it's the one who doesn't apply to get up on the TEDx stage and share your life-changing ideas. Action blocks are slow-motion no-go Hijacks.

In an action block, you've been hijacked by the Part that persistently doesn't do something. It has grabbed the car keys and tossed them into the storm drain—no one is driving anywhere around here!

"But we need to get going—Now!"

As you can probably guess, there is always a second Part in an action block. This second Part feels powerless to make it happen, so it's frustrated and impatient. It often resorts to blaming and shaming you because of how powerless it feels.

Rebellion

For years, Ann was merged with the longing to write and the frustration at not doing it: "I want to write! Why can't I? What's wrong with me?" Barbara spent a lot of time merged with the Part of her that felt disgusted and dismayed because she seemed to be sleeping her life away.

This is a Part that has feelings about the one that is on strike. It is distressed and bewildered by the lack of action. It just wants this whole thing to change.

This kind of Part has developed lots of strategies to get some action going. It tells you what to do in the hopes of getting you moving, such as, "You just need to knuckle down and try harder, get more organized, figure out what the first step is—and just do it!"

Ann's frustrated Part used the threat of deadlines or public humiliation to get her going. Barbara's would either try to bribe her with a juicy reward or lash her with enough scathing criticism to shame her striking Parts into action. It said things like, "You're just weak and lazy" in an attempt to prod her into doing something. The best that happened was reluctant, painful foot-dragging action.

It's a mystery!

There's no real mystery why you put off cleaning out your cat's litter box or changing the oil in your car. Most people find those jobs messy, smelly, and unpleasant. No wonder you don't file your taxes until the last minute, if thinking about numbers and dealing with incomprehensible forms makes your head ache and your stomach churn.

But when it's something you love, that you really want to do, something that would bring you happiness and fulfillment... why don't you do it?

Our friend Chloe loves to write songs for children. Her songs are bright, funny, adorable. She set up a recording studio in her garage with everything she needed to record her songs. But then she got stuck. Day after day, week after week, month after month, she didn't go into her studio. The dust built up, and there were no new songs.

"I don't know why I can't get myself into the studio," Chloe would say. "I really want to. I keep planning to do it. But the time comes, and there's always something else that I have to do."

Part Two: All Tangled Up

You might think you know why you aren't doing it. "I just don't have the time," you might be saying. Or "I don't have enough help." If it's a Tangle, having the time or getting the help won't do the trick. Chloe thought, "If only I had a studio..." And then she got one, and she still didn't record her songs.

If a Part of you gets frantic or anxious enough to try to shame you into taking action, it will come up with self-blaming reasons, such as "I don't have what it takes" or "I've always been a failure and I always will be." Painful—but no closer to being true than "I don't have the time" or "Everything will be great when I have a studio."

If your action block is a Tangle, you don't actually know why you don't do it. So it's a mystery. And if it's a mystery, you can get curious about what's really going on.

Action blocks can untangle—but how?

Recognizing it is a *Part* of you that is *deliberately not acting* can be a huge revelation. That revelation begins the process that unlocks everything.

You want to get started with an exercise program, but you don't. Maybe there's a *Part* of you not exercising.

You need to call your son's teacher to set up a meeting, but you don't. Maybe there's a *Part* of you not calling the teacher.

Ann's writer's block began to untangle permanently on the day she said to herself, "Maybe there's a *Part* of me that doesn't want to write." That change immediately opened up the possibility of being curious, interested, open to knowing more about what was *really* going on.

Barbara's persistent procrastination started to untangle when she became curious about what was going on for the *Part* of her that kept heading for bed.

Tangles transform when you create an inner environment where you are bigger than the Parts involved. You don't try to solve or fix or control what happens. You don't even know what *should* happen. You can simply be curious and open.

Acknowledging the Parts in your Tangle enables you to become bigger than they are. When you become that bigger you, you don't argue or push, agree or disagree with any of your Parts. You don't take sides.

You are there to listen with compassionate curiosity to each of them. You can assume there is some good reason—from the Part's point of view—for this Part to refuse to act. And you can assume there is also some good reason that isn't obvious for other Parts to be critical or upset or pushy.

Tangles stay stuck when you give a judgmental label to the Part that's on strike. Perhaps the most commonly used label for a Part like that is Inner Saboteur. Labeling a Part of you in this way closes down curiosity and compassion. Parts are always so much more than any name we can stick on them.

You don't have to analyze this Part or make guesses about why it's not getting on with it. You'll find out when *the Part itself* lets you know what's going on for it.

Simply say, "There's a Part of me that doesn't make the phone calls." "There's a Part of me that goes to bed during the day." You can also say, "And there is something that is worried about that." You don't need to say more. Making a simple, neutral description of what's happening can be surprisingly grounding and calming.

Then you can begin to develop an empathic connection with your Parts, giving them the kind of attention they need. You are able to listen to what each one most deeply dreads and most passionately wants. Being listened to with this kind of loving attention is transformative for Parts.

When you are able to create a relationship with your Parts that doesn't include any kind of blaming or shaming or good advice or positive resolutions or well-thought-out action plans, things start to change.

Let's see what happened with Ann's writing block.

"On the firing range, down by the targets"

ANN: A few days after I got the wild idea that the reason I wasn't writing might be because something in me didn't *want* to write, I sat down to get curious about that not-writing Part of me. I said, "There must be a Part of me that doesn't want to write, and I'd like to get to know it better."

I knew that it was easiest for me to get in touch with what was going on inside me by sensing in my body. So I closed my eyes and took some time to become aware of my throat and chest and

Part Two: All Tangled Up

stomach. As I continued to sense that area of my body, I said to myself, "I am here to get to know *something in me that doesn't want to write*." And I waited.

After a while, I began to feel something. At first the sensation wasn't very strong, and I needed to be quietly and patiently attentive. It was an odd feeling in my chest. I couldn't describe it easily. Sort of a bending forward. What was it? After a while I realized it felt like I was ducking. Like I was bending over to avoid getting shot at. Wow! *That* was a surprise.

And then an image came: I was on a firing range, down by the targets. No wonder something in me wanted to duck!

A few minutes later, I became aware of a memory from my childhood. I was about six years old, and I saw my father speaking to me with a scornful look on his face. It felt like he was shooting at me. His words pierced me like bullets: "What's *wrong* with you? Who do you think *you* are? The Queen of England? What makes you think *you're* so special?"

The Part of me that didn't want to write was showing me how much it hurt and how scared I felt when my dad fired those caustic words at me. It was showing me that it felt like being shot at. To that Part of me, it was as if the experience of being contemptuously criticized, which was repeated over and over during my childhood, was still going on. It was still being experienced as a *present* danger.

It didn't matter that my father was basically a well-meaning guy—except when he got hijacked himself. From the point of view of the Part of me that didn't want to write, I had better not write a word, or I was sure to get "shot at" again. It also didn't matter how passionately I wanted to write. From the point of view of this blocking Part, keeping me safe from ever being shot at again was more important than anything else.

What happened next

So how did Ann get her writer's block to untangle? Did she explain to the Part that was protecting her from being shot at that her father was dead (which by that time he was) and couldn't hurt her any more? Did she tell it to grow up and get its big girl panties on? No. Those strategies wouldn't have gotten Ann out of her Tangle. They would have been coming from

Rebellion

other Parts, so they would simply have perpetuated the Tangle and possibly even made it more entrenched.

Ann's "on strike" Part had revealed its motivation for not writing when it showed her the memory of her father verbally shooting at her. Ann said to the Part, "I really hear you. I get that you've been protecting me from being shot at. You never, *ever* want that to happen to me again. You never ever want me to feel like *that* again." This is empathy, pure and simple.

After telling the "on strike" Part that she really got what it was trying to keep from happening if she was verbally shot at by her father or someone like him, Ann felt something relax inside her. It was as if the Part was glad it was being understood and heard. An inner relationship between Ann and this Part had been established, and trust was beginning to grow. In Chapter Thirteen, *The Magic of Empathy,* we'll show how you can listen deeply to your Parts so they can trust you.

As Ann spent more time with that Part, she could sense it also needed her to understand something deeper. Pausing and sensing allowed the next layer of the Tangle to emerge. The Part revealed to her that it didn't want her to feel small, inadequate, ashamed, not enough. And as Ann acknowledged each of those feelings, she began to have an uncomfortable feeling in her body. It didn't want her to feel *that*. Amazingly enough, even though it was uncomfortable, it was in no way unbearable. She just noticed where she felt it in her body. She sensed it directly, just the way it was.

Ann said warmly and lovingly to the Part, "Yes, I so get that, *that's* the feeling you've been trying to make sure I never have to feel." She didn't know if anything had changed. Yes, her body felt more relaxed, and a feeling of calm started to spread from her middle. But what had changed in her life?

The very next day, writing was easier. An inner pressure had eased up. She had more of an open feeling through her whole body. She could breathe more easily, and the words began to flow. She found she didn't need to wrestle herself into her chair before she began to write. In fact, it was as if she were being propelled to the chair.

Sometimes something in her would go on a writing strike again, and she would need to turn toward it to see what was troubling it. As she listened compassionately to what it was afraid would happen to her if she started writing, it would relax and release its grip on her again.

Part Two: All Tangled Up

Over time, Ann's writer's block completely Untangled, and she can now write easily. She's up to five books now and counting. Most of them were written with Barbara's help and support—because when Tangles untangle, it's much easier to collaborate with other people. Ann's wish to make a difference in the world through her writing has also come true, judging by the number of people who write to thank her. At the same time, she knows it's not her writing that determines her value and her lovableness.

These days Barbara has no problem getting out of bed to meet the day's challenges. When her feet hit the floor, Barbara says, "Good morning, world." She pauses and looks out her window. When she's in California, she checks to see if there are wild turkeys strutting their stuff or ducks making ripples in the creek. In England, she drinks in the vista spread out across the valley, whatever the weather. She makes lists as reminders, not as something to beat herself up with. Even if tasks still require time and effort, they don't leave her hiding under the blankets for days on end.

And yes, Chloe is regularly recording songs in her home studio.

Chapter 7
INTIMIDATION

Ann didn't tell anyone about her drinking. Even telling Barbara after she had stopped took a big effort. It felt like a humiliating confession. No one, including Ann, knew that Barbara sometimes felt so inadequate and despairing that suicide crossed her mind, until she wrote about it in an article published in 1994[1]. These Tangles felt too shameful to expose to anyone.

We both had Parts of us telling us how inferior we were because of these issues. Ann struggled with an inner voice that called her "weak" and "unenlightened" for her bouts of drinking. Having a nagging feeling that she was a "waste of space" was a familiar accompaniment to Barbara's spells of staying in bed all day.

Tangles are often fraught with harshly critical Parts, that may occur as inner voices or as bodily feelings. Our student Azra wanted to learn web design, but she was stopped by an inner voice that said "nothing will come of it... you'll never be good enough, and you'll just disappoint yourself and others." Jon kept having the feeling that it was too late to try to change his life. "You're too old. What's the point?" was what he heard inside himself.

Having an inner Part that seems determined to attack and undermine you is a tragic aspect of most Tangles. These harsh judgments can be painfully debilitating, especially when you get merged with a Part of you that believes what you're being told.

These criticisms and judgments can be harsh or subtle, and can feel like the voice of Truth.

Recognizing that your self-critical thoughts and feelings are from a Part is the first step to having a different kind of relationship with that Part, a Part some people call the "Inner Critic."

---

1 "The Victim, The Critic, and the Inner Relationship: Focusing with the Part that Wants to Die," *The Focusing Connection,* July 1994

Part Two: All Tangled Up

The illusion of "The Inner Critic"

There is a common view of "The Inner Critic" that it is an awful, hurtful, lying bully and it must be silenced. Recommended strategies for dealing with it include ignoring it, dismissing it, challenging it or overcoming it. "Kick it to the curb." "Just tell it you won't listen as long as it talks to you like that." "Focus on positive thoughts." Calling it "The Inner Critic" makes it sound like a single unchanging and ultimately unchangeable Part.

In Untangling, we have a different take on what's happening when something in you is being critical.

We see being critical as a strategy many Parts use to try to prod you into action or to stop you from doing something. Criticizing is something the Part is *doing*. There isn't just one Part of you that could be called "The Inner Critic," so we call it "the Part of you *that is being critical*," or "the Part of you *that is judging you*."

Parts often resort to being critical and contemptuous when they are in a situation where they feel powerless and anxious. When a Part is being critical, or judgmental, or shaming, it turns out to be motivated by worry or concern about your wellbeing. It isn't your enemy, and if you fight against it, you're identified with another Part—which simply perpetuates the Tangle.

Recognizing when a Part is being critical

Sometimes it is blatantly obvious when a Part is being critical: "You are so messy. It's a miracle you can find anything!" "Look at you! You get any wider and you aren't going to be able to get through the door!" "Get your act together! What's so difficult about getting to bed on time?"

Parts don't only judge what you do (or don't do). They also judge and label what they see as your essential nature. They may call you despicable, contemptible, loathsome, detestable, abominable, awful, heinous, odious, repellent, repulsive, revolting, disgusting, horrible, obnoxious, nauseating, offensive, distasteful, vile, shabby, miserable, disreputable, discreditable, unworthy—or just plain bad.

They are deeply worried that the truth about you is that you are hopelessly irredeemable: "You are a useless failure…" "You are fundamentally broken..." "You are a hopeless mess..." When Ann was in despair over her writer's block, she had thoughts (from a Part) like: "You're such a loser, you can't do anything."

Often a Part will combine these two strategies: "You are such a slob! Look at this place! You really have to shape up and get yourself organized!"

You can feel the effect of being criticized in your body. During those early years of parenting, Barbara had a perpetual stomach ache, a dull heavy pain in her gut. She felt like she was constantly carrying around a huge weight of shame—shame about being an inadequate mother for her precious daughter.

When a Part starts to criticize you, you can easily become diverted by the question of whether you are or are not whatever it is you are being called. But trying to determine whether it is true or not doesn't actually help—inside a Tangle.

Three secrets of criticizing Parts

When we discovered these secrets about Parts behaving critically, we realized we never, ever needed to be intimidated or dominated by our criticizing Parts again. No matter how stern, dominating, or cruel a critical Part may appear, the truth is that it is actually anxious, powerless, and lonely.

They are anxious

The first secret of criticizing Parts is they're primarily driven and motivated by their anxiety. They may be anxious about you and/or the people you love. About whether you are going to be okay. About whether you will be safe and well and protected.

Ann remembers seeing a mother chasing her toddler through the supermarket. The toddler's shoes were untied, and he was dragging his jacket. The mother was shouting, "You're going to fall!" She sounded angry and negative when she was actually deeply anxious and was trying to prevent him from getting hurt.

With your criticizing Parts, it's the same way. They sound negative, harsh, and mean because they are terribly anxious. Your criticizing Parts think that something you're doing (or failing to do) puts you in grave danger. They're worried about your wellbeing, now and in the future. They chastise you for what they believe are your mistakes and misdemeanors in an attempt to prevent something bad from happening to you later—which is what anxiety is usually about.

They are powerless

The second secret of criticizing Parts is that they are powerless to act in the world. They are like backseat drivers. They don't have their hands on the wheel, so they can only say things like, "Go faster!" or "Look out! You're going to crash!" All a criticizing Part can do is say something to you like, "You're such a pathetic failure for not getting your website finished." Why doesn't *it* get the website finished, if it wants it so much? It can't. It's stuck in the back seat.

Criticizing Parts are powerless the way that a parent of a teenager is powerless. As parents of teenagers know, the combination of caring a lot about someone, being worried about them, and being unable to do anything about it often results in judging and criticizing your beloved kid in an attempt to take care of them.

Ann cringes at the memory of the critical things that came out of her mouth back when she was parenting a teenager. One night her daughter stayed out late without letting Ann know where she was. The next day, Ann found herself shouting, "How irresponsible can you be? You're completely and utterly selfish!"

A criticizing Part of us works the same way. It's so concerned about you that it's terrified for you, and there's not much it can do except try to cajole, prod, persuade, and order you (or, more accurately, other Parts of you) into taking the actions it hopes will protect you.

They are lonely

There's one more secret of criticizing Parts, which makes all of this even more intense. It's that a criticizing Part thinks it is all alone. It believes it is the only one that can see the dangers ahead. It feels that the responsibility to save you falls on its shoulders alone. It has been caring for you on its own for years. If it doesn't do this job, it thinks you're doomed. So it must continue, no matter how exhausted it is.

Worse, it has to do the job while being unappreciated. Even reviled and despised. And that makes it, in a word, desperate. Overburdened, desperate, and utterly alone.

Behind the curtain

When you first become aware of a criticizing Part, it probably won't appear to be anxious, powerless, and carrying a lonely burden. It might look and sound like Darth Vader, or a cruel headmistress, or one of your parents on a really bad day. It might say things that don't seem caring at all, like, "You are too old..." "You're completely untalented..." "You're not smart enough to succeed."

But appearance is not the same as reality, as Dorothy discovered in *The Wizard of Oz* when her little dog, Toto, dragged open a curtain to reveal that the raging, fiery head of the Great and Powerful Oz was actually being operated by a stammering little old guy pulling levers. When you get to know what's really going on with the fearsome criticizing Part, you'll find out it's more frightened than you are.

The more vicious a criticizing Part is, the more frightened, frustrated, powerless, and tormented it is feeling. It is hoping something good will happen—or something bad will be prevented—if only it can whip you into shape with its criticism. In other words, it is wanting something really positive for you through what it is doing. Recognizing that it wants to save you can help you to hear what is behind its words.

The power of curiosity

Knowing a critical Part is anxious is the easiest way to shift from being defensive to being curious. Approaching *anything* with curiosity means holding an open mind, not assuming we already know all about it. We can assume instead that there's more we don't know, including why the behavior of that person, or Part, isn't nonsensical no matter how it appears. It's like that for a good reason. It makes some kind of underlying sense—at least from its point of view.

> *ANN:* When I was coming face-to-face with the fact that I had a serious problem with alcohol, the shame of it nearly kept me from admitting I had a problem. I came within a hairsbreadth of not telling Barbara about it at all and keeping the whole thing a secret. Had I done that, you would not be reading this book today. I probably would have stayed mired in my drinking Tangle, and shared the fate of my father, disabled at age 53 and dead thirteen years later from health issues aggravated by drinking.

After I did tell Barbara about my drinking problem, the very fact that she was not disgusted with me was a huge help. She was curious—and that invited me to be curious too.

A Part of me wanted to be drunk, and another Part of me saw the first Part wanting to be drunk as being horribly shameful, unenlightened, and disgusting. But I didn't have to agree with either of those viewpoints. I could say, "A Part of me wants to be drunk, *and* a Part of me finds that disgusting—and *I am here* with both."

Let's see what happens when we assume a criticizing Part is so adamantly harsh and judgmental because it's desperately worried and is powerless to do anything about what it's worried about. If it has a chance to share what concerns it, and be heard, something quite remarkable can happen.

ANN: When I turned with curiosity toward the Part that called me "disgusting and unenlightened" for my drinking behavior, two surprising things happened.

First, my whole body calmed down because I was no longer merged with any of my Parts. I was simply curious.

Second, the criticizing Part was able to tell me what it was so worried about. It had a whole long list. It was worried other people would be disgusted with me. It was worried my health would suffer. It was worried I would end up like my dad.

Because I hid alone in my room when I drank, the criticizing Part was worried I would lose out on the beauty and the juiciness of life. It was afraid I would never look my own life in the eye and meet it with courage and joy.

At this point I realized that the Part wasn't criticizing me any longer. It had started to speak to me about what it *wanted* for me—joy, courage, a more richly beautiful life. Remarkably, the very same Part that had been calling me harsh and judgmental names was now glowing with love for me.

You are not the target

You feel like a punching bag, being called horrible names. You can feel the shame and shock of it in your body, heavy or nauseated or shaky. What the criticizing Part is saying feels true, and you want to run from it, defy it, or sink down under it.

If you've been under attack from a criticizing Part for years, you may be feeling beaten up and battered, intimidated and squashed—the way Barbara felt when she carried around the burden of feeling, "I am a bad mother."

When you feel like this, you are merged with the Part that is being criticized. It feels like you are the target, but you don't have to be. If something in your body feels like it's being punched or kicked or feels sick with shame, you can say kindly to it, "Yes, I can sense how you're feeling. I know it's hard to be talked to in that way. And now I am here."

You don't have to identify with either the criticizing Part or the criticized Part. You can pay compassionate attention to both.

The most tragic love story on earth

We like to say that a criticizing Part loves you, deeply and devotedly, and yet seems doomed to express its love in a way that hurts you. Often a critical Part is totally unaware of the damage it is inflicting. It probably doesn't even think that what it is doing is attacking you. It believes it is saving your life. This could possibly be the most tragic love story on earth… until you help it find a happy ending.

We're reminded of Donna, who took a workshop with us a while ago. Donna had a longing to be a songwriter, but a vicious criticizing Part wouldn't let her take even one step toward her dream. When she thought about writing a song, a harsh, sarcastic inner voice would say, "You? Don't make me laugh! What makes you think anyone would want to listen to something *you* wrote?"

But that began to change when Donna was able to say to the criticizing Part, "What might you be concerned would happen to me if I don't listen to you?" It turned out that Part was worried that she'd be ridiculed by other people if she wrote a song, and it didn't want that to happen to her. When she let it know she heard what it was worried about, it began to relax.

So then she invited that Part of her to let her know what it wanted *for her*. She didn't get a quick answer. She was patient and simply waited. Then we saw her face begin to change. Tears came to her eyes, but not tears of sadness. She was deeply moved. The answer came from a place far deeper

Part Two: All Tangled Up

than anything she had already been aware of: "Oh wow! What it wants for me is to let my own true voice be heard."

It was a profound moment of change for Donna and that Part. It was a Part of her that *loved her*. Her whole relationship to songwriting changed, and she became more free in expressing herself in other areas of her life as well.

Understanding the real motivation of criticizing Parts can completely change how you respond to them. And that in turn can change how criticizing Parts respond to you. When you deeply empathize with this lonely, struggling, anxious Part and listen to its fears and hopes, its anxiety begins to ease, and it starts to trust that it is not alone in caring about your welfare.

When you listen empathically to even the most critical of Parts, there comes a moment when you will spontaneously say to it, "Oh, of course. That makes sense. No wonder you were saying all those awful things to me. I get it." You see its true motivation, underneath the critical things it was saying. You get how it actually was longing to help you be able to live. This is a precious and poignant moment of deep reconnection.

Chapter 8
DESPAIR

B ARBARA: I have spent a lot of my life in some pretty dark places. It often felt like I was living at the bottom of a very deep pit... rain falling on my head... alone and unloved and unlovable. I couldn't imagine feeling free or light or even just okay for more than a few moments. I deeply believed I was never going to have the life I longed for because of some dreadful thing about me that could never be made better. I didn't know what that was, but I could feel in my bones it was true: I was fundamentally flawed.

Over time, I was able to recognize that I was identified with a Part that felt like it was living at the bottom of a pit, and I began to be able to turn toward it. As I turned toward it more and more consistently, the weather swirling above my pit started to change. There were some breaks in the clouds, and occasionally a stray shaft of sunshine found its way into the gloom. However, I still didn't know how to find my way up the steep and slippery sides of the pit and back into the open air.

Even when things started getting better, I would sometimes find myself sliding back down to the bottom of the pit. In fact, the more sunshine there was in my life, the more often I could feel waves of overwhelming anxiety roll in like a thick bank of cloud, obscuring the light. I would have thoughts like: "I'm just kidding myself if I think I'm ever really going to feel happy." And, if I was feeling happy, I would start thinking, "This isn't going to last." In some of my darker moments, thoughts like these would creep in: "What's the point of even trying? Maybe I should just give up. It would be a lot more peaceful than fighting and striving all the time."

When all seems dark and dismal, you can feel as if there is no hope of ever finding your way back into the light. Lost in the dark, you may feel despairing and desperate and all alone. You may struggle not to be overwhelmed by the feeling that just giving up would be best. Keeping

Part Two: All Tangled Up

yourself from being submerged by heavy, hopeless, bleak feelings can take every shred of your strength.

Living at the bottom of a Pit could include all sorts of experiences, not just the ones Barbara went through. Some people feel gray, numb: "Who cares?" Some feel life is meaningless: "What's the point?" Some people experience it as like having a pile of heavy rocks pressing down on their heads. Endlessly ruminating about what went wrong, or feeling awful or guilty or ashamed or disgusted with one's self, are other kinds of Pits. And there is the full-fledged lost-in-the-dark despair.

In a strange way, the bottom of this Pit of despair is where a Part of you may feel most at home. This can be a familiar, almost comforting place where it can hide away from the world.

Pit? What Pit?

There is another more subtle kind of Pit experience that hides underneath false, forced cheerfulness, and denial.

ANN: I never thought of myself as a person who got depressed. When I was growing up, "Be cheerful no matter what you feel or what's happening" was our family motto.

When my father lost his job, and we had to move to a different state, no one talked about how scary and confusing this was. Especially not my mother. When I had dark thoughts as a teenager, I knew I couldn't tell anyone. What I felt, I couldn't show.

Gradually what I felt went deeper and deeper underground, until I wasn't even aware of it. Echoing the words of my mother, I was "just fine."

After I went to grad school, I learned Focusing, and that helped me get in touch with many of the feelings that I hadn't been acknowledging. But there was still a dark underground river of worry and self-doubt that never came to the surface.

Then at age 39 I started getting drunk in the late afternoon and not eating dinner. Over the next five years this happened more and more often until it was three or four nights a week.

I struggled with myself over the drinking, unaware of the feelings that the drinking was helping me suppress. Obsessing about drinking enabled me to ignore the dark, depressed feelings completely.

Recognizing Parts in a Pit

When we started this work, neither of us was aware of the Parts in our Pits. Barbara just felt bad or headed for the chocolate. Ann just got drunk or pretended that everything was fine. Now we know a lot about the many Parts that are often found in a Pit type of Tangle.

In a Pit, there is a Part that feels bad, hopeless, and despairing. It withdraws and tries to hide when things start feeling all too much for it. This is probably the Part most people identify with when they are caught up in a Pit Tangle.

There are a number of other Parts that aren't quite so obvious but are probably operating as well. Some of the most active Parts are those that don't want you to feel bad. There can be several of these, and they can have quite different strategies for trying to get you to feel better.

Some of them try to numb your feelings by using strategies like getting out the ice cream, climbing into your onesie, and watching your favorite movie. Some of them might use denial as a strategy: "I'm fine!" They might tell you that you should count your blessings, sit up straight, pull up your socks and get going! In the Pit there is often a Part that confidently asserts you are an incompetent idiot, a failure, a waste of skin. When you first meet such a Part, it's hard to see what it hopes can be gained from such vicious attacks.

There is often a Part that repeats such thoughts as "I'm a worthless failure" and "I don't deserve to be happy," and another Part that is afraid those awful things are really true about you.

BARBARA: I remember a time when I had been doing Focusing for years, and lots had changed. I felt connected to myself and my authentic feelings in ways I hadn't been in living memory and that was wonderful. However, I still suffered from periods of feeling worthless.

I recognized some things that consistently happened just before I fell into a pit of despair and self-loathing. I would be trying to deal with something difficult or challenging in my life, and I'd feel overwhelmed just thinking about dealing with it. Then I would begin to feel like someone was kicking me in the stomach. It hurt!

Part Two: All Tangled Up

I was most aware of the Part of me that felt bad in my stomach. Years went by, and I still felt overwhelmed and unsure about how to tackle those difficult tasks that needed my attention. And my stomach still hurt.

The big breakthrough came when I realized there must be another Part here that I wasn't aware of, and *it* must somehow be "kicking me in the stomach." I was able to start sensing it was scared that my feeling unsure about how to deal with something meant I was an inadequate, incompetent, useless failure. When I was able to turn toward *that* Part and empathically connect with it, things started to shift.

ANN: I also had a Part that felt bad. But in my case, that Part was completely buried by another Part that didn't want me to feel it. Drinking was only one of the strategies used by the Part that didn't want me to feel bad. I also immersed myself in reading thrillers and romance novels, smoking marijuana, partying, and working all hours. Unlike Barbara, I was completely unaware of having a Part that felt bad. But it was there all the same.

Parts in a Pit can be difficult to recognize. They can feel like you. They can hide in the dark. They can be invisible. They can sound like supportive thoughts or harsh "inner critics."

That might seem like a lot of different Parts. But you don't need to worry about the details. The reason we've told you about all these different kinds of Parts is to help you recognize them so you can more easily dis-identify from them and develop a relationship with them.

"Don't cheer me up!"

There's something counterintuitive that often happens at the bottom of the Pit. A Part that feels like it's living under a dark cloud—despairing, hopeless, depressed, even doomed—actively resists being cheered up. It seems to want to hold onto feeling bad. It pushes back against attempts to show it that things are "not so bad."

This Part is afraid that if it allows itself to be cheered up, something essential will be invalidated and abandoned. It doesn't want something that had already been ignored, pushed away, and buried, year upon year, abandoned yet again. To give in to being cheered up would be a dreadful betrayal of something vitally important. So this Part fiercely resists that betrayal—by hanging onto its dark cloud.

When you can understand and be compassionate to a Part with this kind of motive, it can make a huge difference in transforming the experience of the Pit.

Setting a despairing Part free

There are lots of things we *don't* recommend you do with a despairing Part. Trying to cheer it up. Telling it how lucky it is to have a roof over its head and food in its belly. Getting it to do gratitude practices. You don't belittle or dismiss its experience at all. You don't come up with solutions to the problem. You don't try to fix it. And you don't ignore it.

These familiar and all-too-common attempts to deal with (or avoid dealing with) feelings of despair can help in the short term, and that's not to be sniffed at. But none of them really helps—they don't help either the Part of you that's struggling to survive at the bottom of the Pit or the Parts of you trying to drag that Part back up out of the dark.

So, what do you do? You turn toward a suffering, struggling Part and offer it your compassionate, patient awareness. And you do the same with the controlling, criticizing Part that is making it feel worse. Every Part you meet in the Pit needs your respectful empathic attention, no matter how hurtful or hateful it appears.

Barbara's Pit Tangle began to shift when she realized two important things. First, that there was a Part of her that was apparently trying to throw her into the Pit. And second, that there was a Part of her that wound up suffering at the bottom of the Pit—and that's the one she was identified with.

Over time, Barbara strengthened her capacity to turn toward both Parts, the one saying she was worthless and the one that was suffering. She was able to say to each of them, "I know you are there, and I am here with you." With first one and then the other, she was able to listen compassionately to its pain and its struggles, its fears and its most delicate and fragile hopes. In Chapter Fifteen, *The Healing Power of Love,* we'll show you more about how to give a Part your company in this way.

Part Two: All Tangled Up

Of course there still are times when Barbara feels frustrated and exhausted, but she isn't haunted by painful feelings of being fundamentally flawed. She no longer feels that "hopelessly inadequate and incompetent" is the rock-bottom truth about who she is.

Chapter 9
LONGING

ANN: I was happily married, but I couldn't stop thinking about George, fifteen years younger, who I'd met while teaching a seminar in another country. My attraction to him wasn't logical, and it wasn't even mutual.

I often chatted with George in my head about all sorts of topics, and in my imagination he was always interested, accepting, and warm. Getting an email from him was so thrilling that I started checking for them in the middle of the night, when it was daytime where he lived. My fantasies about seeing him again were fed by the crumbs of kindness in his emails.

This went on for years, and all the time it was happening, my marriage was going on normally. When I was with my husband, thoughts of George were not allowed to intrude. It was as if these were two separate universes. In one I lived my daily life, and in the other I escaped in fantasy with an attractive man who adored me and hung on my every word. In my fantasies about George, it somehow seemed possible that there was a world in which he and I could be together—even though that was not a world that actually existed.

BARBARA: I remember a hot summer's day digging up a patch of my parents' lawn to grow green beans and zucchini and radishes. I was with my boyfriend Ben and our friend Tom, and we pushed our spades into the sod, turning the dark soil. Ben and I were living together, but I couldn't keep my hands off Tom.

At first I had been so happy to be with Ben. For two years I floated on serene clouds of love. I believed I had found the love of my life, the one who would heal all ills, the one who would help me find myself, the one who would make me happy after all those years of being numbingly unhappy. Of course that was not to be. What an impossible burden for another person to carry. I can see that now.

Ben and I were together for almost five years. The last two were like slowly being swallowed by the dark. Tom was like warm sunshine in the gloom. It was impossible back then to stop and sense how lost and miserable something in me was feeling. Instead, I reached out to touch the glow that glimmered on Tom's skin and in his hair.

I tried so very hard to stop those little touches, or at least have them be unseen. No such luck. I vividly remember my mother commenting, "You just can't keep your hands off him, can you?" I felt excruciating shame that she had noticed.

Longing for love

As we have said, a Tangle forms when something essential for your life to move forward fully and freely is missing. When what is missing is some kind of loving attention, the result can be a desperate longing for love.

A Part can recklessly search for something it hopes will fill in what has been missing. The pressure to get what it dreams will meet its needs can be overwhelming. This is the territory of secret obsessions, of being lifted up on euphoric highs and plunging into despairing lows.

A longing Part strives to get what was missing, but it can't just go get what it believes will fill in that gaping hole. It is Tangled up in its shame for having needs that can't be met, in its worries about whether its own deficiencies and flaws are the problem, in its desperation to hide its longing for fear it will be rejected again, and many more such difficulties.

Caustic contempt for being "needy" runs deep in the culture many of us live in. Longing Parts learn early on that they will be rejected and shamed if they let their desires show. Other Parts share the belief that the feelings of the longing Part are "too much" and will make you vulnerable. They try to keep those feelings mostly suppressed so you won't be judged, rejected, and humiliated.

In addition to protecting you from being judged by others, Parts are also trying to keep you from experiencing all the painful feelings you might have about missing the love and attention you needed. They are afraid that if you feel those feelings, you will tumble into a bottomless abyss of endless suffering. So they will do everything in their power to keep you from going there.

Longing

The needs of a longing Part are intensely powerful and can affect how you behave and how you are perceived in the world. This creates a terrible predicament for a longing Part.

On the one hand there is intense internal pressure to find healing and live authentically and freely. On the other hand, there is a compelling need for safety.

Sadly, tragically, the truth is that when you are inside a Tangle, even managing to be adored by the one you desire isn't going to get this longing Part of you what it really needs. Unless the original experience of lack can be directly addressed, all these yearnings and pursuits will always fail to bring real satisfaction and relief.

Hijacked by a Part longing for love

In the movie *Ladies in Lavender,* starring Judi Dench and Maggie Smith, two aged sisters rescue a young Polish musician who has been shipwrecked near their seaside cottage. The sister played by Judi Dench falls in love with this beautiful young man forty-five years her junior. She becomes obsessed with him, simpers and blushes in his presence, shows jealousy when her sister is around him, and hides from her sister her plan to teach him English. It's a classic Hijack by a Part longing for love.

When you are inside the Tangle and have been hijacked by a Part longing for love, the emotions of your longing Part rule you and your actions. You are swept up in them. You have become one with your longing Part. You can't tell whether your feelings and your behavior are appropriate and grounded in reality.

A criticizing Part may be saying, "This is ridiculous, this is embarrassing, this has got to stop." But the longing Part hangs on fiercely to its desires. Another Part probably supports the longing one, insisting that the world is a place where even the most unlikely things can occur. Other people's Parts might join your longing Part and encourage it in its search for someone who will come and make everything better.

Some examples of where a longing Part may look for love and salvation:

- A guru or spiritual teacher—who is seen as the font of all truth and wisdom

- A mentor, therapist, or friend—who is put on a pedestal as someone who can do no wrong
- Someone adored, romantically or otherwise, as the source of all that is good and who will be able to heal all your wounds
- A philosophy or creed or political cause that is seen as the answer to every problem in the world

Because the longing of this vulnerable Part can be so strong, it can be prey to charlatans and con-artists.

Some signs you have probably become hijacked by a longing Part:

- You lash out in anger if anyone questions your feelings of love or attraction for someone or something.
- You feel overwhelmingly ashamed if someone notices how you feel about someone or something.
- You feel euphorically hopeful or even absolutely certain you are finally going to get what you are longing for.
- Or, conversely, you are terrified that what you long for is impossible to have, or doesn't exist, or you are the kind of person who won't ever get it.

If you find yourself overwhelmingly and magnetically attracted to someone or something that hints at or even outright promises to heal you and make you happy—a person, a job, a place, even an idea—then most likely a longing Part has taken over.

The three faces of a longing Part

There are three main ways longing Parts show up when you're merged with them. They may be euphoric, convinced that they have found the answer, their true love, their guru, their savior. They can fall into deep despair, believing they will never get what they want. Or they may become enraged that they have been disappointed, let down, betrayed yet again, and that they are being blocked from getting what they so desperately want.

When a longing Part is euphoric

When a longing Part feels its core issue has a here-and-now chance of being healed, it may respond with a surge of energy and hope, carrying you away on a tide of ecstatic feeling and action.

Barbara remembers when she was newly in love with her first husband. She was certain she had met her true soulmate. Her friends told her, "You sound really crazy!" but she didn't care. She now believes she was being swept away by a longing Part in its belief that she had finally found the one who would make her happy and whole.

Ann "fell in love" in her forties with a British rock star and was obsessed with him for five years without ever meeting him. She listened to his music constantly and came to believe they were communicating with each other on some level. Anyone who wanted to remain friends with Ann during this time—including her husband and Barbara—could not express any doubts about the reality of this "relationship."

A euphorically longing Part is likely to be not only jubilant at the possibility of getting what it is longing for, but also terrified that its chance for fulfillment will be snatched away—again. Everything will be filtered and interpreted through these hopes and fears. The Part is likely to be so preoccupied by these feelings that it cannot see or hear what is actually happening now. Imagine someone with their fingers in their ears and their eyes firmly shut. The Part is afraid it will be talked out of wanting what it wants or stopped from getting what it hopes will make everything better.

One way a longing Part deals with this anxiety is by becoming rigidly certain that it will get what it wants. Blind and mulish insistence in the face of contrary evidence is a strong indicator that you are identified with a longing Part.

A person merged with a longing Part can be so single-mindedly obsessed with something or somebody that no one else matters, including close friends. Ann remembers times when she would have thrown any of her friends under a bus for a chance to be with the beloved one she'd never met. That is how strong these feelings can be.

When a longing Part falls into despair

In the middle of this kind of Tangle there will be at least one other Part frightened about you becoming merged with a longing Part. A criticizing, controlling Part is probably deeply afraid that who you *really* are is nothing but a bundle of babyish needs—and that the grown-up you is just a fragile facade that will crumble, revealing you to be a shamefully spectacular disaster of a human being. When that Part keeps whispering how crazy you are to imagine you can get what you truly want, a longing Part can collapse in despair.

A longing Part can believe that it is true what criticizing Parts are telling it, that it doesn't deserve to get its needs met. It can decide that means it can never get what it needs or wants.

When a longing Part gives up the last tiny shreds of hope it has been clinging to, it can become overwhelmed by disappointment, lost in its suffering. It can feel as if all the joy in the world has drained away, and you are living in perpetual gloom. Empty, numb, half dead.

When a longing Part becomes enraged

Euphoria can turn to rage when a longing Part feels thwarted or rejected. When those rosy, glowing dreams are shattered, a longing Part is left in a turmoil of disappointment and frustration. When those feelings are combined with fears that there is actually something terribly, horribly wrong with you, it can be excruciatingly painful.

A longing Part may blame others for the crushing of its chance to get what it has always needed. Its fury can even build until it explodes in violence. This may be the only way that a longing Part can feel it has any power at all.

We are not saying that anger is bad. Anger is an important emotion. It can be a protest against something that is not right and a sign that your boundaries have been violated.

However, the rage of a longing Part is boundless and does not resolve or heal even if it is expressed. It is wordless, physical, visceral. This is the kind of rage that—in its most extreme form—can kill.

A longing Part transforms

So what do you do when you are caught up in a longing Part's euphoria and exuberance? Or when you are trapped in a downward spiral of a longing Part's despair or about to be swept away in the red mist of its rage? You cultivate your inner resources so that you can keep company with your longing Part without becoming merged with it.

When this happens, the longing Part will be grateful you are there. The missing relationship this Part has been longing for all this time is one you can provide. When you are present as your whole self, you'll be able to say to the longing Part: "I am here with you now."

Over time, with this kind of inner love, the longing Part does transform.

ANN: My crushes on unavailable men continued until I was able to spend time compassionately with a very young Part, longing to be loved, at the core of my Tangle. What a relief it is, now, to be able to form connections with both men and women that are simply what they are, here and now, without the aura and glamor of unrequited and inappropriate longing.

BARBARA: A Part of me longed to be loved and cherished. I wanted to be seen as special in an attempt to compensate for feeling unloved and unseen. One result was that I fell in love over and over again. When I wasn't dreaming about someone and wondering if maybe this time he would really see me as I truly was—and still want me—I was sinking into a kind of despair about being unloved, sure I would be alone forever.

What changed, after Ann and I developed the Untangling method, was that I became able to simply and directly experience feeling unloved and unseen, without becoming overwhelmed by the pain of it. I was able to sense it exactly as my body still carried it, held it, lived it. Simply sensing how all of it felt in my body without fighting it or fearing it, without believing it made me an inadequate, inferior, hopelessly flawed human being, without merging with it or identifying it as "me."

Even though I had been suffering a great deal of emotional and physical pain for years, I had not sensed it in this way before. Over time, this way of directly sensing how that Part of me was carrying those painful experiences made it possible to have a completely different kind of relationship with myself and everyone else in the world. Now I don't need to be loved and told I am special in order to feel okay about myself.

Is all love and devotion just the feelings of a Part? Actually, real love is possible, and so is real admiration for a teacher or dedication to a cause. So what is the difference between being in a loving relationship and being merged with a longing Part that's trying to find salvation? A longing Part, even when euphoric, has an underlying air of desperation. A longing Part

Part Two: All Tangled Up

is trying to fill in something that was missing, such as Barbara wanting someone to tell her she was special and approve of her totally, to avoid the pain of not feeling seen and loved as she is. Real love includes seeing the person you love as they actually are, being able to confront them when necessary and forgive them when they need your forgiveness. It also means being openly vulnerable and authentic, willing to take responsibility for what you say and do.

A longing Part is seeking fulfillment of its need for a kind of relationship that was missing when the Tangle first formed. Those early relationships are no longer present, and the next steps of life that were needed are still missing. Yet transformation is possible now.

When you can provide the loving, empathic company that is still needed, your longing Part no longer has to be alone in that impossible situation. In Chapter Fifteen, *The Healing Power of Love,* we will show how you can be there with it, giving it loving, empathic company. This is profoundly and remarkably healing.

PART THREE
THE POWERS OF PRESENCE

Before the step this part of her was stuck, silent, hurt, resentful, refusing to live, and that was all that could be felt. Now as this part of her comes to be sensed more, the wanting in it stirs, moves, and speaks. Now its wanting flows forward into being felt and lived.

Eugene Gendlin, *Focusing-Oriented Psychotherapy*, p. 37

In this section of the book, we'll take you through the whole Untangling process, showing how you can create the environment of transformation for your own Tangles. You'll make the remarkable discovery—as we did—that what you think is the biggest problem in your life is actually your greatest source of strength, freedom and joy.

Untangling has five Powers. We call them the *Powers of Presence*. We will describe all five of them in Chapter Ten, *The Environment of Transformation*, and then we'll show you each of the Powers again in detail.

You may want to try out each one as we describe it to you, or you may want to read this whole section through without trying out the processes for yourself—yet.

Part Three: The Powers of Presence

Chapter 10

THE ENVIRONMENT OF TRANSFORMATION

When 8-year-old Ann showed up for third grade at the small, rural school in western Illinois, feeling odd and out of place and different, what happened next did not have to become a Tangle. Being bullied by the other kids, being laughed at for wearing the wrong clothes, hearing taunts that she was "ugly" and had "germs"—she could have come through those times with her self-esteem intact if someone had seen what was happening and helped her. But that was not how it was.

There are thousands of difficult, painful and challenging things that happen in life. Many are beyond anyone's control. But even big, painful events can be a source of growth if you have what you need so you can work through the situation.

Your Tangle formed because a certain kind of environment was missing which meant something in your life got stuck. When the kind of environment you need is missing, your organism puts experiences that are "too much" into a kind of deep-freeze. To help you manage and survive the consequences that follow, Parts are created.

It is never too late to provide the kind of environment that was missing when your Tangle formed. If a living process has been stopped, it can always resume when the conditions in the environment enable it, no matter how long that takes.

Untangling lets you become the environment of transformation where what has been frozen can thaw. This allows that stopped process to start again so the spontaneous, natural right next steps of your life occur.

Self-in-Presence

Early in our work we began to notice something interesting: We needed to pay attention to how we were paying attention. The quality of our attention affected whether something stuck was able to shift—or not.

Tangles are full of Parts. In order to help them shift and untangle, we needed to cultivate a way of being that wasn't "partial." Rather than taking sides or having an agenda, we needed to be interested and curious toward every Part.

We call this way of being *Self-in-Presence*.

Self-in-Presence is you when you are not merged with any Part. As Self-in-Presence you turn toward and stay with what you are feeling—or, as we say, what Part of you is feeling.

You recognize the Part and acknowledge it, creating a space in your inner world where it can be just the way it is. You develop a relationship with it, and you do this with each Part of you that needs your company.

Sometimes it can be challenging to turn toward a Part, such as one that is in a great deal of pain or one that is behaving in a self-destructively out-of-control way. If so, you become aware that something in you is finding it challenging, and acknowledge that Part of you as well.

As Self-in-Presence, you are the environment where every Part of you can be welcomed and related to just as it is. As Self-in-Presence, you give your Parts what they have been missing. You become the environment in which your Tangle untangles.

The Five Powers of Presence

Over the years we have identified five processes that work together to create this transformative environment. We call these *The Five Powers of Presence*. These Powers can be learned, applied, developed, and strengthened over time. All of them together make up the Untangling method.

- *The Power of Cultivating Self-in-Presence*
- *The Power of And*
- *The Power of Deep Empathy*
- *The Power of Felt-Sensing the Stoppage*
- *The Power of Felt-Sensing It All*

We'll say a bit more about each one here, and look at each of them in depth in later chapters.

The Power of Cultivating Self-in-Presence

We've shown you how easy it is to become merged with Parts—to be hijacked or taken over by them. Staying present as yourself and not getting caught up in the struggle between Parts is a huge challenge in a Tangle. Probably at some point you will wind up getting merged with frustrated and despairing Parts or Parts trying to solve and fix your life.

Self-in-Presence is what is needed. When you cultivate Self-in-Presence, you are shifting from being inside your Tangle to being able to have your Tangle without being caught up in it or overwhelmed by it.

The Power of Cultivating Self-in-Presence enables you to be present as yourself and keeps you from being overwhelmed even when the strongest and most difficult feelings arise. Learning to cultivate a state of Presence means you will be able to come back to your self even after you have been taken over by a Part.

As you develop your ability to cultivate Self-in-Presence, you will become confident in knowing what to do when you feel confused, numb, desperate, thrown around, fragile, vulnerable, upset, at the end of your rope. In other words, you will be able to recognize when you are merged with a Part and know how to unmerge from it.

Cultivating Self-in-Presence is a skill, an ability you can strengthen, like a muscle. We will show you how to cultivate this spacious state of welcoming awareness. When you consciously and deliberately cultivate Self-in-Presence, you will be able to fully experience what you feel without being merged with it. And you will know that, despite all that is going on in your Tangle, *you* are fundamentally okay.

The Power of And

As we've seen, a Tangle involves many Parts. *The Power of And* creates a space where more than one Part can be acknowledged at the same time. You can become comfortable with the experience of having many Parts, even though they are likely to be at odds with each other. You become able to welcome all aspects of a Tangle respectfully, in a way that each and every Part of you can be included.

As you develop *The Power of And,* you will learn not only how to accept multiple Parts at once, but also how to detect hidden and invisible Parts and create relationships with them too. You'll discover that liking or preferring one Part over another—or disliking one Part more than another—shows you there is yet another Part in your Tangle that needs to be acknowledged and welcomed.

The Power of Deep Empathy

The Power of Deep Empathy enables you to offer each Part the exact kind of empathic company it needs. This makes it possible for a Part to reveal its hidden fears and longings. When it is met in this way, it can soften, shift, and ultimately release the energy and abilities that have been entangled in that Part. The Part melts back into your whole self again, making all its attributes freely available.

Ever since your Tangle formed, many Parts have devoted a great deal of their energy and creativity to keep you from feeling what is at its core. They have been terribly afraid you would be overwhelmed if you directly experienced what is there.

With *The Power of Deep Empathy,* you'll give those Parts the kind of company they need so they can start to relax and trust you to be the calm, strong Presence they long for you to be. As those Parts start to trust your strength and stability, they step back so you can directly experience what was frozen when the Tangle developed.

The Power of Deep Empathy is essentially cultivating a relationship of compassion and curiosity with each of the Parts in your Tangle. In the process, you'll connect with your deepest truths, experience emotional healing, and receive the positive life energy that has been bound up in your Parts, energy that has been unavailable to you until now.

The Power of Felt-Sensing the Stoppage

Every Tangle has a Stoppage at its core—a way in which it is utterly impossible to live freely. With *The Power of Felt-Sensing the Stoppage* you go deep. You directly experience the core of your Tangle in a new way.

You do this by feeling the Stoppage directly in your body. Your body still "has" or "carries" the experience of the Stoppage—in the muscles and viscera of your physical being.

In *The Power of Felt-Sensing the Stoppage,* you sense this stuck process as a bodily experience. You notice where you can feel this in your body and then precisely symbolize what it feels like, with images and metaphors, gestures and sounds. When the symbols accurately match what you are feeling in your body, the Stoppage will spontaneously transform.

Amazingly, any stopped process can start again, just as a river long frozen flows freely when it thaws. This can happen at any point in your life, no matter how long it has been since it first became frozen. It's never too late.

The Power of Felt-Sensing It All

A Tangle includes not just your own personal history. It also includes how your Tangle is involved in your present life. In *The Power of Felt-Sensing It All,* you go wide with your awareness, sensing the whole of the Tangled situation and everything (and everyone) it includes.

Just as in *The Power of Felt-Sensing the Stoppage,* you describe this sense of the whole as precisely as possible, using words, images, and metaphors. When the symbols fit precisely, fresh aspects of the situation emerge, and new ways of living in situations that have been stuck become possible. Whatever form the newly released energy takes, its forward movement will enhance your life.

So how do Tangles Untangle?

Untangling is the process of practicing all five *Powers of Presence*. This is how you create the environment in which transformation of your Tangle happens.

As your Tangles shift and loosen, you may feel immediately better, calmer, more peaceful, more able to take a wider view. You may feel you are being freed from constrictions you thought were going to be there forever.

Sometimes you may feel more uncomfortable. You may experience emotions and memories that you have kept under wraps for a long time. Discovering how you have been unaware of much that has been driving and determining your life can be upsetting for Parts of you. In the chapters that follow, we will show you how to meet these upsets if they occur. You'll probably experience a combination of all these reactions, from time to time.

As you get to know your Tangle better, and as you encounter it more and more deeply, you will be exercising the five Powers of Presence over and over again. As you become adept at using the Powers, they will blend together

Part Three: The Powers of Presence

into a seamless way of being with your Tangle. Your Powers will become available to you whenever and however they are needed in your process.

We cannot say exactly what *will* happen, but we can say the changes will be in the direction of your fuller, richer, freer, more authentic life.

Chapter 11
Becoming Your Biggest Self

Trying to shift a Tangle from the inside is like trying to move a rug you're standing on. Inside a Tangle, you're always merged with one Part or another: one that's trying too hard, or one that's wanting to give up, or one that's worried about other people's reactions, or one that's sick of the whole thing—to list just a few of the possibilities!

What you need for your Tangle to untangle is a way to not be merged with any Part. You need a way to be calmly, steadily, warmly present for your Parts with acceptance, strength, and curiosity.

You need to be Self-in-Presence.

The Power of Cultivating Self-in-Presence

Cultivating Self-in-Presence is the most important thing you can do as you explore your Tangles. Being Self-in-Presence will protect you from being overwhelmed, it will give you clarity, and it will keep you on track. Being Self-in-Presence will make it possible for you to give your Parts the compassion, tenderness and understanding they need. It is the environment in which your Tangles can transform. You will need it—not just at the beginning, but all through the process.

Cultivating Self-in-Presence is the most important thing you can do in Untangling.

As you go along, there may be times when you feel discouraged because nothing seems to be changing, and Parts of you might just want to give up. There may also be times when you encounter Parts that feel like scary monsters about to attack you, or dark abysses you could fall into, or some other kind of threat that could harm you. With Self-in-Presence, you will know, no matter how it looks or feels, you are not in danger. Knowing that every Part inside you needs your compassionate presence, you will be able to turn toward the Parts of you that are scared as well as those Parts of you that seem so scary.

As you feel yourself being embodied, calm, curious and courageous, you are living, breathing Self-in-Presence. As you create a safe environment for whatever needs your attention, you are creating a world of Self-in-Presence.

Does all that seem like a tall order? Sure, being Self-in-Presence isn't always easy. That's why we talk about *cultivating* Self-in-Presence. Being Self-in-Presence at any given time is always a work in progress.

Self-in-Presence itself is not a feeling, it is a way of being present for your feelings. And your Self-in-Presence isn't something separate from and bigger than you, like God or Divine Spirit or Universal Good. Self-in-Presence is you. When you are Self-in-Presence, nothing in you is bigger than you are. You are the space in which everything in you can be the way it is.

Language that supports Self-in-Presence

Language can be amazingly powerful. Language can hurt, undermine, diminish, block. Language can also heal, liberate, uplift, and support. We have crafted language that can help you shift from being merged with a Part into being Self-in-Presence and being *with* a Part. In Inner Relationship Focusing, we call it *Presence Language*.

You might have the idea that you have to feel compassionate first in order to relate as Self-in-Presence to your Parts. Actually, just using the language of Presence, whether you feel compassionate yet or not, helps you to cultivate Self-in-Presence.

Something in me...

The first important phrase of Presence Language is "something in me." This phrase helps you to unmerge from a Part.

When you say "I am angry!" you are merged with a Part of you that is feeling angry, with all the emotions, thoughts and world view of that Part.

When you say, "*Something in me* is feeling angry," you are already more than just the Part that is angry. Now you are not angry; a *Part* of you is. You can feel you are more than that angry Part, and, because of that, you can be present to that Part, listen to it, be empathic, and keep it company. It was not possible for *you* to be present for the angry Part when, for all practical purposes, you *were* the angry Part.

When you unmerge from a Part, you still feel that Part's feelings. They are still there—in fact, maybe you feel them even more fully than before. You haven't pushed them away, denied them, gotten rid of them, or repressed them. But you can also feel that you are more than any of those feelings.

By shifting your language, adding just three words, "something in me," you can shift to being Self-in-Presence in relation to Parts in your Tangle.

Try this:

Pick an emotion you are aware of in your Tangle.

Make a short sentence that includes that emotion. You don't have to get into the reasons or the causes. Three words are enough. For example, "I feel angry" or "I am worried."

Now, take your sentence, for example, "I feel sad," and change the word "I" to *"something in me."* Like this: "I feel sad" becomes *"Something in me* is feeling sad."

Notice what happens. Sense what that feels like in your body now.

When people use this language, they often report a greater lightness, space, and curiosity. They find themselves being compassionate and warm toward something they previously didn't want to feel.

Part Three: The Powers of Presence

"I am sensing..."

"I am sensing..." is the second powerful phrase that helps you to unmerge from your Parts and move toward identifying with Self-in-Presence. When you say "I am sensing," you are identifying with the larger "I." *You* are the "I" that is sensing. You are the "I" that can notice a Part and listen to it. You can be a steady and compassionate presence for all your Parts.

Laurence, a student of ours, attended a community meeting, and someone unexpectedly called on him to give an opinion. He froze in terror. He felt sick and wanted to run from the room. He managed to mumble something he thought sounded totally inadequate. Later he felt ashamed and disgusted with himself and viciously criticized himself for being so "pathetic."

Then he remembered what he had learned about Self-in-Presence. He realized that the surprise of being called on to speak in public had thrown him into the middle of his Tangle. Just recognizing this brought a bit of relief. He paused, and then became aware of a Part of him that was worried that when he had to say something in public, he would open his mouth, and nothing but gibberish would come out.

He said to himself, *"I am sensing something in me* that is worried that anything I say will be gibberish." Just saying those words brought Laurence a deeper breath.

Then he became aware of a sad, heavy feeling in his heart. *"I am sensing something in me is feeling sad..."* It took a few minutes of sensing what was there for more words to come. "Oh... it's sad because I am a person who loves language, and at times like that words fail me." His eyes felt moist, and he gently put his hand on his chest.

Presence Language helped Laurence to un-merge from his Parts and to begin to relate to them. He felt more relaxed and more connected with himself. His mood shifted. Of course, his Tangle had a lot more Untangling to do, but this much already made an important difference.

> Take the sentence you got before: for example, "Something in me is feeling sad."

Now add the words "I am sensing" to the beginning of your sentence.

"*I am sensing* something in me is feeling sad."

Notice what happens. Sense what that feels like in your body now.

Self-in-Presence is cultivated

Self-in-Presence is a way of being that you can practice and cultivate. It isn't something you have to go looking for somewhere else, or someone else you need to turn yourself into. Self-in-Presence is not an object inside yourself that you have to search for, find, and hang on to. Self-in-Presence is *you*.

But sometimes you are merged with a Part. When that happens, you see the world through the Part's eyes. You can't see the larger picture or another person's point of view. The feelings you have when you are merged with that Part are shaped by its fears and desires. This is why the first and most important step in Untangling is to cultivate Self-in-Presence.

Cultivating Self-in-Presence takes practice. You will get better at it with intention and attention. Over time, cultivating Self-in-Presence will become second nature, part of your way of living your life.

We have found three ways to reliably cultivate Self-in-Presence:

> **Recognizing** is noticing you have become identified with a Part. This is actually a big thing. Recognizing that you've become identified with a Part is already a huge step away from being stuck inside a Tangle.
>
> **Resourcing** is deliberately caring for yourself as a way to strengthen your ability to be Self-in-Presence. It's something you can do at any time. It can be as simple as stopping to smell the roses. It can be as challenging as making sure you get good sleep and food and exercise when your life is full of commitments. And it is something you can do in the middle of a Tangle when you need to find Self-in-Presence again.

Part Three: The Powers of Presence

Relating is the practice of connecting with your Parts with curiosity and empathy. When you say to a Part, "Hello, I know you're there," you become the one who said hello. When you relate with kindness to something in you, you are bigger than it is. Simply relating to a Part of you is already a way to cultivate Self-in-Presence.

Recognizing

ANN: When my partner, Joe, griped at me for not being able to hear him, I merged with an irritated, frustrated Part of me.

My chest felt tight. Thoughts like *He's the problem! If he just spoke more clearly I'd be able to hear him just fine!* swirled in my head.

"Yeah, well, you mumble!" I snarled at him.

"I do not..." he mumbled back at me.

Argh! I could feel my temperature rising. This was going to descend really fast into one of those "You do!"—"I do not!"—"You do so!" kinds of arguments if I didn't do something different. Thankfully, because of all the work we have done in Untangling, I recognized I was merging with a Part of me that was feeling infuriated with my beloved partner.

How did I recognize I had become merged? I noticed how tight and uncomfortable I felt in my chest. I noticed how infuriated I felt and that I was blaming Joe for how I was feeling. I realized I had just snapped at him—which is not how I wanted to be with him.

And what became possible because I recognized I was merged with a Part of me?

I was able to take steps to regain Self-in-Presence. I paused and took some time to sense my body and just breathe. I took a moment to look out the window at my favorite tree.

Then I acknowledged *something in me* was triggered. "I am sensing *something in me* is furious with Joe right now... " I turned toward the Part of me that had snapped, silently saying to it, "I can sense how furious you are with him right now."

Within a minute I had recovered my sense of humor and my curiosity. I wanted to reconnect with Joe from my open heart, so I asked for a hug... and got one. We were able to talk calmly about how both of us have more hearing challenges as we're getting older, and what we can do to be kinder to each other.

"I'm merged!"

If Ann hadn't had a fair amount of practice in regaining Self-in-Presence, this little encounter with Joe would have been messy for a lot longer. (It has happened!)

Although this story may seem like a fairly simple example of getting merged with a Part and how you can use Recognizing to start recovering Self-in-Presence, we want to point out something important. If you don't recognize you are merged with a Part, it is almost impossible to unmerge from it. That makes recognizing and acknowledging when you are merged tremendously powerful.

As you develop and strengthen your ability to cultivate Self-in-Presence, you will notice more and more often when you are merged with something. You may even start to feel as if you have spent your whole life identified with Parts. Something in you might get quite upset about that. You can recognize *that* Part of you as well.

Recognizing and acknowledging Parts is a prerequisite to everything else you do in Untangling. As soon as you become aware you are identified with a Part, *you* are already bigger than the Part you have been merging with.

Let's look at some typical signs that you need to cultivate more Self-in-Presence. We are not judging any of these feelings or situations as wrong or bad. We are inviting you to notice whether these happen in your life so you can more easily recognize when you are becoming merged with a Part.

Getting hijacked

Maybe you have Parts that do things like scrolling on your phone for hours or smoking or eating too much. Or Parts that can't seem to stop working or trying to please others.

You can often recognize a Part like this because you feel helpless to control or stop it. (It's actually another Part of you that's feeling helpless!) We explored this type of Tangle in Chapter Four, *Hijack*.

Part Three: The Powers of Presence

Maybe you have important phone calls you need to make, but day after day they wind up getting put off. Or you have a symptom that worries you but you don't make that appointment to go see your doctor. You might have a creative project you want to get on with, but there is always something "more important," and months go by with nothing more done on it. We explored this kind of Tangle in Chapter Six, *Rebellion*.

Uncomfortable body sensations

Hungry? Tired? Tense? Maybe you really are. But in a Tangle, those kinds of sensations can be how a Part is feeling. Parts can have many body sensations. Stomach aches, headaches, tense aching muscles—a Part can feel all these and more. Sometimes a Part can even find it hard to breathe.

Barbara remembers how for years she had a kind of burning, churning feeling in her stomach. She thought it was just indigestion so she mostly tried to ignore it, or she fed it, hoping that would calm it down. When she finally learned how to relate to it directly, she discovered it was a Part of her feeling almost unbearably anxious.

Caught up in beliefs

Your thoughts about the Tangle are part of the Tangle. Often these thoughts are stated as if they are self-evident facts. Some of these are beliefs that Parts of you hold about who you are or about what the world is like. They may be beliefs about who or what is to blame for your Tangle. They can be completely contradictory.

Ann's Tangle about drinking included both a belief that her drinking wasn't actually a problem, and a belief that it was a terrible problem that was too shameful to tell anyone about.

One of the most common beliefs in a Tangle is: "This will never change." You can see what a big effect such a belief would have on how you are likely to approach your Tangle. These beliefs are held by Parts—and when you unmerge from those Parts, you also unmerge from their beliefs.

Feeling judged

When you feel criticized and become defensive, you have become merged with a Part that is feeling judged. Feeling guilty, embarrassed, and ashamed are some other signs of being merged with a Part that feels judged.

Obsessing

You might keep thinking about something you've done or not done. You might keep telling the same story over and over again. When you can't get a painful thought or memory out of your head, or when you can't stop obsessively doing something, you can recognize that a Part of you is deeply anxious.

Feeling triggered or activated

What is commonly called "being triggered" is, in our terms, being taken over by a Part. Body feelings of being triggered can include your face feeling hot, your breathing feeling tight, and your heart pounding in your chest. You may feel ashamed or enraged, overwhelmed or terrified.

Feeling overwhelmed

You might feel overwhelmed by your emotions. You might feel that life is just too hard, too difficult, too much. You might feel overwhelmed by the intensity of the sensations you have in your body. Feeling you are at the mercy of your emotions is a sure sign that you are merging with a Part.

Feeling bored or flat, feeling "nothing"

The experience of feeling blank, empty, bored, flat, "just going through the motions" is probably an indication that a Part of you is damping down or shutting up another Part of you. You're merged with the one doing the repressing, and the other Part is in there somewhere.

Not being able to see someone else's point of view

Parts find it difficult to be empathic. Holding rigidly to your own point of view and being unable to be open to someone else's point of view is a sign of being merged with a Part.

Losing your sense of humor

Parts in a Tangle often take everything extremely seriously. They are tense, anxious and pushy. For them, life is hard. When you feel grimly self-righteous, without even a glimmer of a balanced perspective or sense of humor, you are undoubtedly identified with a Part.

Part Three: The Powers of Presence

Practicing Recognizing

Recognizing when you are merged with a Part is an ongoing process. The more you do it, the better you'll get at it.

You can practice noticing your body sensations, your thoughts, your emotions, and the actions you are taking so you can more and more easily spot when you are drifting away from Self-in-Presence.

When you pause for a drink of water, you can notice how you are feeling in your body. When you take a break to stretch and look out the window, you can ask yourself, "How am I right now?"

Being merged with a Part doesn't mean you are some kind of bad or inadequate person. Recognizing you are merged is not at all like spotting failure so it can be improved. That would be grim! No, recognizing Parts is an act of kindness. It allows you to turn toward Parts that are showing up in this way so you can offer them compassionate care and understanding.

Resourcing

Resourcing is deliberately having—or remembering—experiences that enhance your ability to be calm, present, relaxed, open, and energized. When you are Resourcing, you are helping yourself to have what it takes to be available for the Parts in your Tangle in the way they need. Here are seven suggestions for Resourcing:

Notice what's happening right now

When you're tangled up in Parts, you're often full of anxious thoughts about the future or painful feelings from the past. This is why being simply aware of the present moment can be a powerful way to resource yourself as Self-in-Presence. Look around, notice what draws your attention in your environment. Notice the sounds, the smells, the feel of the ground under you, what you can sense right now.

Get into your body

For most people in most situations, feeling grounded in the body is a great support for Self-in-Presence. (Exceptions might be if you are in physical pain or if your body feels unsafe to you.)

If you need some help to be able to feel your body from the inside, wiggling your toes can be a quick and easy way for you to do that. If you're sitting, you can sense the pressure of your body on the chair. Standing up, stretching, or shifting your position can also help you to feel your body.

Take time to become aware of the support of whatever is under you: chair, floor, ground and the support of your hips, pelvis, feet, back.

Many people are helped to ground themselves by becoming aware of their breathing. Notice the feeling of the air moving through your nostrils and down into your chest. Sense how your chest and belly expand and contract as you breathe.

If you feel like you hurt all over, it can be very helpful to be aware that not absolutely all of you is in pain right now. You might take time to notice if there is *somewhere* in your body that feels at least neutral. It might be your toes or the tops of your thighs. Hold that in your awareness while you also acknowledge how uncomfortable (or even painful) everything else is feeling right now. It strengthens your Self-in-Presence "muscle" to hold both of those experiences in your awareness at the same time.

Feel what feels good

Many of us are used to noticing our bodies only when they give us trouble, like when we have a headache or backache. It is worth taking a bit of time to become aware of more pleasant body feelings.

Notice whatever feels open, alive, flowing, warm or good in some way in your body right now. Welcome whatever feels alive, even a little bit. (Acknowledge whatever doesn't feel that way, too. You are not choosing; you are open to it all.)

"I am the space"

BARBARA: I remember a time long ago, before we had started creating this work, when I was overwhelmed by a Part of me that was sobbing its eyes out over unrequited love. My stomach hurt. I felt a painfully strong pressure all through my torso. It felt as if the pain was going to go on forever.

I was able to acknowledge it and even say hello to it, but the pain in my stomach didn't really change. After getting through the best part of a box of tissues, I decided to call Ann.

After listening patiently, Ann suggested that I sense how much space all that needed. Almost immediately I got the image of a white stallion that needed all of Montana to run in. As I imagined being as big as Montana, the feeling in my body transformed. It immediately eased and became spacious, open and free.

Ever since that experience, we have known that "the space that I am" is not limited by the boundaries of the physical body. Often, emotions that feel as if they are being held in a small space inside the boundaries of the physical body can be sharply uncomfortable. When they have more space, there is relief.

You might wonder if your emotions would become overwhelming if you gave them more space. Perhaps some Parts of you are afraid that will happen. But we can't recall a time when emotions that were given more room while being held by Self-in-Presence ever became overwhelming. When *you* as Self-in-Presence give Parts the space they need, you are still always bigger than they are, no matter how big they get.

You are likely to feel a stronger sense of being present as your steady, resilient self when you say to yourself, out loud or silently, "I am the space where all that is in me can be as it is." You really *are* that space, and in that space there's no need for anything to change. Think of it as "expanding to include" rather than "pushing away."

Draw on memories of Self-in-Presence

Remembering times when someone was there for you, and what that felt like, is one way of connecting with how it feels to be Self-in-Presence. Another way is to remember a time when you were able to be steady and strong when a friend needed help. You showed up. You were there when your friend needed you. Perhaps you held the hand of someone who was suffering, and your actions said—with or without words—"I am here with you."

Draw on the qualities of Self-in-Presence in others

You can also recall the qualities of someone you admire for their calm and generous presence: past or present, fictional or real, a spiritual being (Buddha, Kwan Yin, Jesus) or someone like a beloved grandparent. Pause and savor the feeling it gives you to think of that person and the qualities in them that you treasure.

Draw on memories of nourishing experiences

Are there times when you have felt calm, strong, more fully yourself? Hiking in the mountains? Sitting by a stream? Having tea at your local café? Listening to your favorite music? Laughing with friends?

When you need to cultivate Self-in-Presence, you can draw on your memories of nourishing and supportive situations, and let the feelings inspired by those memories come to be resources for you now.

For Ann, having her daughter's dog fall asleep on her lap is one of the sweetest, most peaceful feelings on earth. She can draw on that memory when she needs those peaceful feelings the most.

Barbara remembers standing up to her knees in a deliciously cool summer lake when she was six years old. That was a long time ago, but the memory, vividly recalled, is still extraordinarily resourcing.

An example of Resourcing

Our friend Liza was going through a hard time. Just as she and her husband were returning from the first vacation they had dared to take since the pandemic began, they learned that their 34-year-old son was in the ER. His kidneys were failing, and the doctors didn't understand why.

Liza was the main person available to ferry her son around to his doctors' appointments and be his emotional support. The stress and worry started to wear on her. Once she cried all day. The next day she was angry, yelling at everyone who came near her. She was depressed. She woke in the middle of the night and had trouble going back to sleep. That made the next day even harder.

There's nothing surprising about being stressed—and distressed—under such circumstances. But Liza could tell that her emotional state was getting in the way of her being able to be there for her son.

So she consciously cultivated her resources. She made use of a whole set of self-care activities that made it more possible for her to be Self-in-Presence, even in the midst of this scary and uncertain time.

At various times during the day—and at night when sleep was elusive—Liza made a practice of pausing... getting in touch with her body... putting a hand on her heart... and asking, "What feels good and right?"

When she did this at night, the answer might be, "Well, I'm breathing. I'm warm, I'm in my bed, my body is supported." Then she would pause to receive that. "Yes, that's true. And this is how it feels when I take in what's good."

Liza also kept her commitment to writing in her daily journal. There too she started by noticing what felt good and right. Doing so gave her more ability to turn toward the tough feelings that needed attention. In other words, doing so gave her more Self-in-Presence.

Liza's Focusing partnerships were important as well. She told us, "When I'm very much in the grip of my Parts and overwhelming emotions, being with a Focusing partner makes all the difference. They can hold the space for me. They can accept me as I am. They can be quiet with me." Other people's Self-in-Presence can support our own.

Being Self-in-Presence doesn't make hard feelings go away. But it can make it possible to know that under those feelings, we are fundamentally okay. That's what Liza told us. "It's hard. I'm acknowledging that. And I do know that, even though it's really hard, I am okay."

Putting Self-in-Presence "in the bank"

Your capacity for Self-in-Presence is not an all-or-nothing kind of thing. It fluctuates from moment to moment and situation to situation. Resourcing builds this capacity, making it stronger. There will be times when your ability to be Self-in-Presence is challenged. But those times will come less frequently and be shorter in duration as your capacity grows.

We highly recommend making Resourcing a part of your daily life by building in supportive activities that become new habits, and by taking time for special experiences that bring you pleasure and joy. Even something as routine as brushing your teeth and washing your face can strengthen your resources. Don't underestimate the power of the mundane.

What are your favorite ways of nourishing yourself? What is your go-to Resourcing activity? What new ones might you experiment with?

- Walking, dancing, or doing karate?
- Maintaining a practice like Focusing or yoga or meditation?
- Hugging?

- Spending time with a friend?
- Getting into water—swimming, showers, baths, spas?
- Listening to music?
- Napping?

You don't have to wait to do Resourcing until you are stressed or challenged. Resourcing lets you build your reserves of Self-in-Presence so you have calm, spacious awareness when you need it. Taking good care of yourself day by day is an important way to strengthen your resources and Self-in-Presence. That can restore you after a difficult day and fortify you for tomorrow. Resourcing can, in effect, put Self-in-Presence "in the bank" for a rainy day.

Relating

ANN: I was sitting in a plane on the runway in Milwaukee, Wisconsin. The skies were stormy, the plane was small, and my anxiety about turbulence was at maximum intensity.

My stomach was clenched, I was sweating, my heartbeat was drumming in my ears... and we hadn't even started to move!

So I decided to try what we teach. You know, as a last resort, try the thing you teach others to do!

I put my hand on my stomach and I said, "I am sensing something in me is really scared right now." I waited. There wasn't much of a change but I could feel it was now just a tiny bit easier to breathe. I knew this was a step.

Next I said to the feeling in my stomach, "I really hear how scared you are. And I am here with you."

I waited a few seconds to let my words sink in. I wasn't aware of any change this time. So I said it again. "I really hear how scared you are. And I am here with you."

After saying the words, I sensed again... Are my words being received?

No, not yet...

The third time I said the words, there was a change. And not just a small release. In fact, my stomach totally relaxed.

Soon after that, the plane started to move. We took off, up through the clouds. The flight to Chicago wasn't the smoothest I've ever been on, but my stomach stayed relaxed the whole time.

No matter how many times we teach this, and no matter how many times I do it myself, it still feels like a miracle how relating to something I am feeling can make such a difference.

Cultivating Self-in-Presence through Relating

So much happens in relationship. We offer and receive comfort, kindness, and support. We collaborate and co-create. We laugh and cry together. We discover and change together. We are born into relationship, and without relationship we can't develop. We can't even learn to communicate without somebody there to communicate with.

Just as outer relationships are important, so are our inner relationships. Many of the insights and recommendations in this section are from Inner Relationship Focusing, which is the version of Focusing that we have been developing.

Your Parts and your Tangles exist because of failures in *relating*. When a Tangle first formed, no one was able to give you the kind of attention and care you needed to move past the disruption in your life that you were faced with. What your Tangles need now to help them untangle is an *inner relationship with you*. When you are kind, compassionate, and curious with your Parts, relating to them from Self-in-Presence, you are taking essential steps needed to live beyond your Tangles.

What we find really amazing is this: You don't have to be kind, compassionate, and curious before you start relating to your Parts in a way that helps them heal. It can work the other way around. You can start relating to your Parts... and that can in itself cultivate Self-in-Presence. Here are some ways to do that.

Acknowledging

Once you have recognized a Part, acknowledging it is there is the simplest step you can take toward having a relationship with it. "Acknowledging" is not yet making direct contact with it. It's more like recognizing someone you see on the other side of the road.

Acknowledging alone can make a profound difference. However you are feeling, you can say to yourself, "I can sense this is here and *this* is what it feels like right now." And from there you can move toward deepening your connection with it.

Making contact

Once you have acknowledged something, it's time to make contact. It's like waving to that person on the other side of the road, and then seeing if they'd like you to join them.

Making contact with a Part is a process of developing a relationship with it. The kind of relationship you have with each Part depends on what *it* needs. Some Parts will want you to be close, some Parts will want lots of space. Some Parts love when you say "Hello!" to them. Some Parts will disappear if you are that direct. Every Part is individual and has its own unique needs for connection and relationship. You'll learn how to take your time to sense how each Part needs you to be with it.

Here are some ways you can make contact:

- Sense how something in you needs you to be with it
- Say, "Yes, I know you're there," or say hello to it
- Simply be with it, keeping it company attentively and silently

Getting curious about what life is like for it

The next stage of developing your relationship is empathically sensing what life is like for this Part. This is not how *you* feel about it, but how *it* feels. Empathizing with a Part is like empathizing with a friend. You can often tell how a friend is feeling even when they don't feel like speaking.

Part Three: The Powers of Presence

Because a Part is part of you, it is possible to tune into how it is feeling through sensing how it feels in your body. Sometimes this takes a while, but as you spend time with it, you can sense that this Part is scared, or sad, or tired, or whatever it is feeling.

Some Parts seem more like thoughts. They tell you what terrible things are going to happen to you. Or they tell you what a bad person you are. Those kinds of parts are hard to feel in your body, especially at first, but you can still become aware of their point of view. It is important not to either dismiss them as distractions or get into arguments with them about whether what they are saying is true.

This kind of Part is worried or anxious about something. In order for it to be able to shift, you need to really get how things are for it. You need to listen below the surface meaning of what it is saying, allowing it to reveal the hopes and fears that are motivating it.

Your Parts need you. They need your company. They need a relationship with you. What was missing when your Tangle first formed was a specific kind of relationship. Learning how to foster Relating with your Parts is fundamental to providing that kind of relationship now.

The first, essential step to Untangling is allowing whatever is in you (emotions, reactive states, memories) to be as it is. When what is in you can be as it is, then change becomes possible.

The fastest, surest way to start cultivating Self-in-Presence

As you go forward through this book, there is one thing we would like you to remember.

If you start to feel overwhelmed: Pause. Pausing is always the first step.

When Liza feels a crying jag coming on, she pauses.

When Ann feels like biting off her partner's head, she pauses.

When Barbara gets the urge to eat something and she's not sure she's actually hungry, she pauses.

Pausing allows you to Recognize when you've become merged with a Part of you. Pausing enables you to connect with your environment, your body, and your breath and start Resourcing. Pausing also lets you turn toward and begin Relating to one of your Parts.

Home ground

Self-in-Presence is powerful. You are not overwhelmed. You are not denying. You are aware of your experience as it is. You are acknowledging it.

When you have and acknowledge your experience in this way, things change. You do not need to do anything to your problems or yourself in order for transformation to occur. This may be hard for you to believe, but it's true. When you are Self-in-Presence you are the environment in which change occurs spontaneously and organically.

When you plant carrot seeds in your garden, you don't have to tell them how to be carrots. That, they already know. What you do need to do is provide the environment for them to fulfill their carrot destiny. It's the same with you. Self-in-Presence provides the environment in which you can fulfill your own unique destiny.

Of course you will not always be in a state of Self-in-Presence. Your capacity to embody Self-in-Presence can be undermined by lots of ordinary challenges that have nothing to do with Tangles. Perhaps you had a terrible night's sleep. You might have a cold, and your brain feels like cotton wool. It might be the end of a long, frustrating day, and you're ravenous.

In other words, your state of Self-in-Presence is always in flux, constantly influenced by a multitude of factors. Perhaps the most important factor impacting Self-in-Presence is if the situation you are in is Tangled. Inside a Tangle, maintaining Self-in-Presence is hugely challenging. That's why it's worth the time—in fact it's priceless—to do Recognizing, Resourcing, and Relating whenever you need to, as you go forward with Untangling.

The good news is, if you are struggling to be Self-in-Presence, just recognizing how challenging you are finding it is already a step toward being Self-in-Presence more fully again. You're always one acknowledgement away from being more Self-in-Presence... and that can make all the difference.

Part Three: The Powers of Presence

Chapter 12
ALWAYS ROOM FOR ONE MORE

BARBARA: It was hard living most of my life in a body that didn't feel like mine. I would look in the mirror and feel disconnected from the person looking back at me. When I caught a glimpse of myself reflected in a shop window or looked at photographs, I would wonder who is that fat woman? Would I ever be able to feel comfortable in my body and be happy with what I saw in the mirror?

In my struggles with my weight, I have bounced, ricocheted and ping-ponged back and forth among a multitude of strategies for dealing with my excess pounds. From the very strict Mayo Clinic diet when I was 19 through to the Big Is Beautiful ideology of my 40s, I tried either to get rid of my extra pounds or to come to a place of acceptance with them.

I'm not sure when it all started. The genesis of lifelong inner wars can be subtle and hidden. I remember not liking my legs when I was about eight. I started comparing them to Nancy's and Shelly's long thin legs. I wanted legs like theirs, because clearly long legs were beautiful. (Actually, I was delicately thin myself—but short.) I started to feel ashamed of my legs and tried to hide them. It wasn't long before I started to control my eating—and also lose control of my eating. Back and forth, with each passing year, the war over the control of my eating grew in intensity.

Each side in the war was stubbornly determined to prevail. One side was trying to make sure that I ate well (but not too much) and exercised ("I'm just telling you what you already know to be good for you!"). The other side was feeling controlled, resentful, deprived and disregarded—and it knew where the chocolate was. After all, it bought and hid it in the first place! It wanted to ensure I had the freedom and pleasure it felt I deserved and had support from some other Parts that said it shouldn't matter what I weigh. "I am not a number on a scale! I should be able to be loved no matter how overweight I am. I am smart and valuable even if I am fat." Of course, all of that's true—but it's not the point.

The battles between different Parts in a Tangle can be ferocious and seem like life-and-death. On the surface the warring Parts can appear utterly in opposition. It can seem as if the only way to resolve conflicts like this is to simply choose a side and get rid of the other side—or at least get it under control.

But for a Tangle to untangle, something different from choosing sides is needed. Every Part in an inner conflict needs to be welcomed without bias and given the kind of attention it actually needs.

Parts, Parts, Parts!

In a Tangle it often feels like there's a lot going on and it's all snarled up together. You've lived for a long time with your Tangle being unseparated, a whole heap of undifferentiated stuff. It can be tricky to recognize when there's more than one Part in a Tangle. If you have been merged with a Part in your Tangle for a long time (and most of us have been merged with our Parts for years), any Part you are merged with just feels like you.

As one of our friends told us: "I'm so busy, the only time I can read my emails is late at night. Then I feel I have to stay up to deal with them. Then I'm so exhausted I can't sleep until I stuff myself with mac-and-cheese. Then I wake up unhappy with my body and feel like I need to spend time at the gym, which takes even more time. I'm longing to live a different kind of life but I don't have a clue where to start." Lots of different Parts, right? The sheer number of different feelings and thoughts competing for your attention can be disconcerting and overwhelming.

As you have probably already realized, being Self-in-Presence when you are entangled is a lot more complicated than just unmerging from one Part. Tangles are tangled because there is more than one Part active *at the same time*. Sometimes you are aware of only one of these Parts, while others hide in the shadows. When you are immersed in your Tangle, it can be hard to see what's going on.

In addition, Parts are usually locked in conflict with each other about many things, including what's going on, how you should feel about it, and what you should do. All of this makes it hard to know what your right next step is. Sometimes you're merged with one Part, agreeing with another, and fighting with yet another as each of your Parts tries to deal with the difficulties and challenges in your Tangle—all at the same time.

This is where another Power of Presence will help a lot. It's called *The Power of And*. When you start to notice how Parts are entangled with each other, you can also begin to create some space and breathing room for all of them.

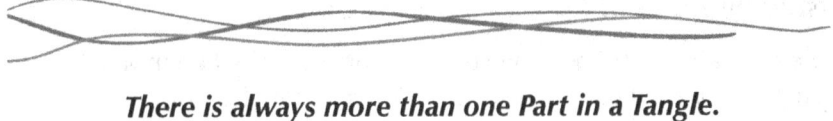

There is always more than one Part in a Tangle.

Tangles are complex—always. In a Tangle, there are many voices, many sides to the story, many Parts pushing and pulling against each other. For your Tangle to resolve, there has to be a way of including every Part of you. *The Power of And* is a simple and straightforward way of doing this. It has a structure that is easy to learn and remember.

The Power of And

In the first Power, *Cultivating Self-in-Presence,* you learned how to Recognize when you are merged with a Part. We showed you how to become a welcoming, stable presence for your Parts by Resourcing. And we showed you how to unmerge from a Part and begin developing a relationship with it by Relating to it.

Now we are going to show you a way to cultivate and maintain Self-in-Presence even when there are many Parts—as there always are in a Tangle.

What's new in *The Power of And* is that you—as Self-in-Presence—are present with all your Parts, holding them all as having equal worth, and not merging with any of them. As you practice *The Power of And,* you grow in your capacity to be the space where all the Parts in your Tangle can be welcomed just as they are. This inner environment of inclusion without bias is a powerful incubator for transformation.

As you practice *The Power of And,* you strengthen Self-in-Presence. Over time and with practice, it gets easier to welcome your Parts with equanimity, without taking sides or becoming merged with them.

This is a big deal!

Part Three: The Powers of Presence

The language of And

In *The Power of And,* our recommended language is a way to relate to multiple Parts without merging with any of them. As you might guess, the word "and" is a key element.

Listening for "but"

Here's an easy way to spot when there is more than one Part in your Tangle. Listen for the word but when you describe your Tangle.

- "I want to finish writing this chapter *but* I just keep putting it off."
- "I want to lose weight *but* I keep on eating until I'm stuffed."

Do you see what happens when you say *but?* Two Parts are pulling in different directions. Noticing when you say *but* can help you spot two Parts in conflict. When you've noticed you have two Parts set against one another by the word but, you can simply change *but* into *and* to help you shift away from inner conflict and toward holding both equally.

- "I want to finish writing this chapter *and* I just keep putting it off."
- "I want to lose weight *and* I keep on eating until I'm stuffed."

Do you notice what a big difference it makes when you simply change *but* into *and? But* divides and dismisses. *And* connects.

Presence language on both sides of And

You learned how to say, "Something in me ..." to help you unmerge from a Part. Now, let's use that language to unmerge from two Parts, so you can be with both of them.

- *Something in me* wants to finish the chapter **and** *something in me* keeps putting it off.
- *Something in me* wants to lose weight **and** *something in me* keeps on eating until I'm stuffed.

If you are trying this with something in your own Tangle, notice if saying it like that makes a difference. You probably feel there's a bit more space for each of those Parts. You might even start to feel curious about what's going on for each of them.

Creating an And-sentence

It can help to consciously create a sentence that includes all the Parts you are aware of right now. Start by saying, "I am sensing something in me..." as you describe a Part. Then welcome another Part by using the word *"and."* Follow the word "and" by saying "I am sensing something in me..." and then describe the next Part you are aware of.

Remember Laurence, who had a Tangle about speaking in public? At first, he expressed it this way: "I want to let my voice be heard, but I am so petrified at the prospect that I feel nauseated even thinking about it."

Using the language of *The Power of And,* he constructed a sentence that started with "I am sensing something in me _____," followed by "and," followed by "I am sensing something in me _____".

Like this: *"I am sensing something in me that wants to let my voice be heard, **and** I am sensing something in me that is so petrified at the prospect that I feel nauseated even thinking about it."*

When Laurence created his *And*-sentence and said it out loud, he was amazed. Even with such a small change in language, he felt more clear, with more inner space, not so dominated by his Tangle. He wasn't taking sides. He was acknowledging both Parts in him without choosing which one was right or telling the truth or was the "real" him. Doing that freed up a lot of energy.

A feeling of relief and clarity naturally happens when both sides in a Tangle are equally acknowledged.

All the Ands you need

Often when you acknowledge two Parts you become aware of another one. Excellent! Just add it to your sentence with the word *And*.

When Laurence said, "I am sensing something in me that wants to let my voice be heard, *and* I am sensing something in me that is so petrified at the prospect that I feel nauseated even thinking about it," he paused while he felt some relief and clarity.

Then he exclaimed, "I am so tired of this!" He realized this was being said by another Part that had feelings *about* his Tangle, so he included it in his *And*-sentence as well.

Part Three: The Powers of Presence

His new *And*-sentence was: "I am sensing something in me wants to let my voice be heard, and I am sensing something in me that is petrified and nauseated even thinking about it... *and* I am sensing something in me that is so tired of this."

Feelings about your Tangle—about what it means about you or the world, about what is possible or about what is going to happen to you—all these are aspects of your Tangle and belong in your *And*-sentence as well.

One of the great qualities of the word "and" is you have all the *ands* you need. You can always add another one. There is always room for one more guest at the table.

Yes, your sentence might get rather long! You might want to write it down so you don't have to try to remember it.

Laurence's sentence eventually became:

"I am sensing something in me that wants to let my voice be heard...

"*And* I am sensing something in me that is petrified and nauseated even thinking about it...

"*And* I am sensing something in me that says I'm too sensitive and I should just get over this...

"*And* I am sensing something in me that is so tired of this whole struggle...

"*And* I am sensing something in me that is afraid this is never going to change."

Each time that Laurence became aware of another Part and added it to his *And*-sentence, he felt more spacious and more able to turn toward his Parts.

Creating a spacious welcome

When Laurence felt he had named all the Parts he was aware of so far, he added something more: "*And* all of them are here... and I am here with all of them. I am the space where all of them can be as they are."

"And all are here..."

This phrase welcomes and acknowledges everything within your awareness. You can even welcome Parts that you only have a vague sense exist somewhere in your Tangle.

Sometimes it's obvious. Perhaps you can sense only one of them at the moment, and the rest are hiding. Perhaps one of them is clearly calling for your attention. Or perhaps all the rest point to one of them and say, "Go be with *that* one first."

Sometimes when you turn your attention to one Part, another one jumps in and starts to attack it. All right... that means the attacking one needs to [be with] first. At least until it calms down!

Once you sense which Part needs your attention first, you will be ready to take the next step of empathizing deeply with that one—and then with the others still needing your attention. It helps to clearly communicate to both (or all) your Parts that they are respected and valued and will get their turn to be heard... if not today, then soon.

"...and I am here with all of them."

Adding these words to your *And*-sentence points to the relationship you are going to cultivate with each Part that needs your company. At the end of your *And*-sentence, say: "And all are here... *and I am here with all of them.*" (If there are just two of them, you'd say "both" instead of "all.") This brings you into the picture and helps you to experience your own presence in relationship with all your Parts.

"I am the space where all of them can be as they are."

Remember Barbara's discovery that she could be as big as Montana? Your experienced body, which is your body as you experience it from the inside, is as large as you feel it to be.

Inspired by Barbara's experience of being as big as Montana, we created the sentence: "I am a big enough space where all of my feelings and Parts can be as they are."

Through *The Power of And*, you can become the space where all your Parts can be welcomed and you can turn toward any of them with curiosity and compassion.

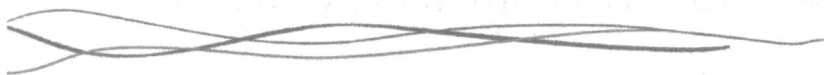

The Power of And

1. Include yourself as Self-in-Presence by starting the sentence with "I am sensing..."

2. Refer to each of your Parts as "something in me..."

3. Connect each Part in your sentence with the word "and."

4. To include all of the Parts say, "And I am here with all of them."

5. To help you create a welcoming environment, say, "I am the space where all of them can be as they are."

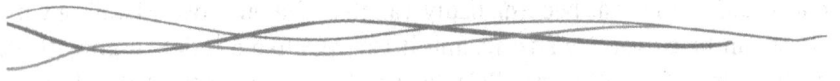

Too many Parts?

"I am finding so many Parts," one student told us, "I'm feeling overwhelmed."

"Ah," we said to her. "Perhaps there is something in you that thinks you have to keep track of them all."

"You mean I don't?"

No, you don't. Keeping track of all your Parts isn't part of the job. You can trust that the Parts that need your attention will call for it.

There may seem to be lots of Parts but this is not the time for sorting them out. Later they will probably sort out into two or three main "sides."

You may discover that what you thought were two or three Parts are really all the same Part. And sometimes you might realize that what seems to be one Part is actually two closely entwined Parts. But for now, you can simply include whatever is in your awareness.

So let there be many Parts, if that is how your Tangle emerges. You can be a mansion with many rooms, or a huge field with lots of space, for all of them to live in.

Welcome the whole crowd: "Hello! I am here with all of you."

Bias and partiality

Do you feel you have to choose between Parts? Do you have a need to decide what is better or right or true? Maybe you like the one that feels more alive or more free or you prefer the one that seems more pleasant or feels safer in some way. Perhaps you are drawn to choose the one that's more like the kind of person you feel you should be. Or you don't like the side that feels dark or scary, or the one that reminds you of, say, your mother or father.

When you take sides in a Tangle, you often do so because one side feels more right (or true or good or valuable) than the other(s). But it's not you taking sides, it's a Part of you that is choosing one side over another.

In a situation that has become badly Tangled, the pull toward siding with a Part can be extremely strong, and it can feel like a relief to go with it. But this kind of relief is actually a dead end. At a deeper level nothing has actually changed. You are still inside the Tangle.

BARBARA: One of my *And*-sentences is: "I want to paint, in me feels that everything else is more important." that I prefer the Part that wants to paint. You migh I said "*I* want to paint." I know that painting makes

But knowing that does nothing to resolve the T I'm Untangling, I need to treat even something true and as self-evident as my desire to paint, a

So I need to create a sentence that includes three Pa wants to paint *and* the Part that feels that everyth important *and* the Part that prefers the one that wa

Here's my *And*-sentence: "I am sensing somet wants to paint *and* I am sensing something in me thing else is more important *and* I am sensing that prefers the one that wants to paint."

It's important to notice when you are leaning toward som it over another Part. Or leaning away from it—wanting to it or suppress it. It takes a lot of conscious intention no impulses and instead to recognize and make space for ev

Acknowledge there is a Part of you that has feelings *ab* you—ah, yes, that's there too. Then you can be with the the Part that has a bias. You can be with all three of th curiosity.

Self-in-Presence doesn't take sides. Choosing one side c stop the process dead in its tracks. As Self-in-Presenc to choose between them. You can safely assume that al tribute something important to your life as your Tangl

What needs my attention now?

You've acknowledged the Parts in your Tangle that connected them with the word *and*. Now what?

In the next Power you'll be developing a deeper and m with each Part that needs your company. Because yo to know all your Parts at the same time you'll need them is first.

Chapter 13
The Magic of Empathy

A friend of ours told us about going into a hospital as a volunteer aide. When she arrived at the children's ward, a 5-year-old boy was having a meltdown. He had just learned he wasn't going home that day, and agonized cries of "I want to go home!" echoed through the ward. His mother, nurses, and aides were all trying to offer him games or toys—"Look, sweetie, you can play with this!"—but he was inconsolable.

Our friend knelt down right in front of him so she had his attention for a moment, and in a clear warm voice she told him: "You want to go home!" She didn't try to distract him. She didn't try to take his feelings away. She just met him where he was.

He stopped crying, looked at her, and gave a deep sigh. And that was it. He turned to his mom and let her give him a hug and a toy. No more tears.

Empathy is "getting how it is" for someone. It is meeting that person where they are. Experiencing their world through their eyes, their mind, their feelings without judgment or analysis or advice. Just getting what they are up against and how they are attempting to deal with that.

Being "got" is something you may never have experienced. Many of us have rarely been heard for how it actually was for us to deal with the struggles, anxieties, and challenges of our lives.

Usually somebody was trying to get us to feel differently or was giving us advice about what to do. Even with the best of intentions, this kind of help isn't particularly helpful.

When you are met with real empathy, something remarkable happens. In a kind of alchemy, what was unclear becomes clearer, more distinct, more differentiated. What was hard-edged and unchangeable starts to open up and become flexible. You can begin to explore. You have realizations and discoveries that weren't possible before. You go deeper. You find yourself saying things like: "I thought I was angry at her, but actually... I can sense how something in me feels disappointed and kind of sad."

Part Three: The Powers of Presence

Your body relaxes. You have space to be more *you* than before. Being empathically met can change everything.

The Power of Deep Empathy

So far, with *The Power of And,* you took some time to acknowledge a number of different Parts—probably more than you thought were there at first. And we hope you felt some relief at just having acknowledged that they are there.

So here you are with all these Parts. Now what? How can you interact with them in a way that takes you out beyond the boundary of the Tangle... not just going around in the same old frustrating circles? This is where *The Power of Deep Empathy* comes in.

Tangles are entrenched, repetitive, cyclical patterns. Most of them have been in place for many years. Attempts to figure out a Tangle—or break out of it—are doomed to fail, because you just wind up thinking and doing the same things all over again in a different guise.

What *does* work? Cultivating Self-in-Presence, acknowledging the Parts, and then offering a particular kind of empathy to each Part.

The Power of Deep Empathy enables you—as Self-in-Presence—to keep company with your entangled Parts so they are deeply met and understood. You will be creating a space of time and attention where each Part can be met just as it is right now.

You will be doing your best to get how it is feeling, how it sees the world and what matters to it. You will be sensing its deepest fears and longings—the real reasons it feels and thinks and behaves as it does. When a Part knows you get how it is for it, it radically changes.

The truth about Parts

A Tangle is a problem, but it wasn't created to cause you trouble. Even though it probably doesn't seem like it, your Parts have been trying their best to help you stay alive and do well. They've all been trying to enable you to live as fully as possible, as safely as possible, within the limits imposed by their own deep-seated fears and by what you were up against in your life.

These Parts of yours have been doing their best to keep you safe and maintain your integrity, sometimes for most of your life. Often they have been rejected and reviled, both by other people in your life and by other Parts of you. Each of these Parts has been struggling valiantly on its own and is still soldiering on, still trying to protect and save you from the threats it sees.

Even Parts that don't seem to be helping—even Parts that declare nastily that they don't care about you in the slightest—will turn out to be on your side when you connect with them deeply and empathically. It just takes a bit of time.

Anybody who works so hard for so many years on your behalf deserves to be appreciated. That goes for your Parts too. The more you are able to recognize and value how diligently your Parts have been working for you, the more they will open up to you. The more you hold a welcoming, caring space for them, the more they will be able to relax.

Crucially, what these entangled Parts need is relationship. Now you are able to provide the most important relationship of all—a relationship with *you*. In the process of empathizing with a Part, you will forge the kind of relationship it has always needed, in which it is accepted, validated, understood, accompanied, trusted, respected, and loved. In other words, it needs a relationship with *you* as Self-in-Presence.

A radically different approach

You already know the surface level of your Tangle only too well. This is the level where you are bored to tears by talking in circles about it. It is the level where you are sick to death of feeling those same old emotions. It is the level where your thoughts replay themselves in a tediously endless loop. It's like being stuck in a maze with no exit.

At this superficial level of a Tangle, Parts try to figure out what to do (or think or feel). We want you to recognize how amazingly creative all your Parts have been! Their strategies are *functional*—they have purpose. They are never simply random.

They have developed patterns of behavior and habits and belief systems that have worked remarkably well despite all their imperfections. These strategies are the best your Parts have managed to come up with.

Part Three: The Powers of Presence

Unfortunately, as you already know, their strategies do not untangle the Tangle. They actually keep the Tangle tangled—because they are incomplete, partial solutions that bump up against and compete with the different strategies used by other Parts. It's heartbreaking, really. So much well-intentioned striving and energy goes into these intrinsically inadequate strategies.

Engaging with the strategies of Parts at this superficial level will get you nowhere. Everything you do to try to solve or fix a Tangle from inside the Tangle just perpetuates the Tangle.

Something radically different is needed.

You need a kind of process that will take you beyond the boundary of your Tangle. You need a process that reveals what is going on beneath the surface of a Part's strategies and at the same time, allows something new to happen.

The depths of dread and desire

It turns out that each and every Part in a Tangle has deep-seated fears it has been trying to cope with, all on its own, for a long, long time. Each Part also has hopes and dreams for your life that it has been holding onto for an equally long time—hopes and dreams it has been striving desperately to fulfill.

Every Part has deeply held fears and hopes for you.

Fears and hopes are two sides of the same coin. When you don't want to die, you want to live. When you don't want to be insulted, you want to be respected.

On one side a Part is fixated on something it is trying to prevent happening to you, and on the other side are its dreams of what it hopes will turn the sky radiant blue and bring joy into your soul.

However, because this is a Tangle, having empathy for a Part's fears and desires isn't simple to do. If you just ask a Part what it wants, at best it will tell you its strategies for getting what it wants. For example: "I'm asking it what it wants, and it says it wants me to pull myself together and work harder."

For things to shift, you need a way to go below the superficial level of a Part's strategies to its bone-deep fear and heart-held longing. Okay, well and good, but how do you actually do that?

This is where *The Power of Deep Empathy* comes in. Yes, you can understand your Parts in a cognitive way, and that can be valuable. But far more important is for them to know that you are there, for them to feel you empathizing with them. And this in turn will allow them to trust you enough to let you know how they are feeling, what they believe, and what they most dread and long for.

Settling down to listen

Our student Grace told us about being one of two non-white people in her first grade class in a middle-class suburb in New Jersey. She was mocked for her skin color and for the shape of her eyes, and rather than seeing her as someone with her own abilities and interests, people simply assumed that she would be good at math.

In her family, she was expected to be a good, submissive daughter. She was taught to stay small in order to be safe in the dominant white American culture.

By the time she was in her mid-20s, Grace had two graduate degrees, had traveled the world on her own, and was living in New York City working in the corporate world with a six-figure salary. But nothing she did took away the feelings that she should stay small and that she was somehow wrong for being Asian.

Cultural messages and beliefs are embedded in many Tangles. This, of course, includes racial, sexual, and other cultural stereotypes. You might think that a Tangle would be impossible to shift unless those beliefs shift in the culture. But actually, Tangles threaded through with culturally held beliefs can shift—as we will see.

Grace sat down to spend time with her Tangle about feeling she had to keep submissively quiet and stay small, no matter how much she achieved.

Part Three: The Powers of Presence

Through *The Power of And,* Grace became aware of three Parts in her Tangle. One was a Part that did everything it could to keep her small, using messages like, "Keep quiet! Nobody wants to hear what you have to say!"

Another Part, equally strong, constantly pushed against those messages, urging her to do more: "Get bigger! You haven't done enough! *You* aren't enough!"

A third Part didn't say anything, but quietly wanted to resist and rebel against both of these messages. It wanted her to be herself… somehow.

With *The Power of And,* Grace was able to acknowledge that all of these Parts were there, and that she was there with all of them. She wasn't merged with any of them. She was ready for the next step.

Grace took some time to sense which Part needed her attention first. It became clear it was the one that constantly pushed her to do more.

When you are starting to have a relationship with a Part, you can't just rush in and start interrogating it. That wouldn't get you far if you did it with another person, and it won't help with a Part either. So the first thing Grace did was take time to sense how that Part was responding to her attention.

It might have felt angry with her or cautiously optimistic that she would give it the respect and attention it needed. It might have wanted to communicate a lot right away, or it might have wanted silence and quiet company.

In fact, in this case, it was feeling a bit wary. She could feel that this Part wasn't sure its point of view would be respected.

Building trust

In order for your Parts to trust you, you need to be willing to keep them company just the way they are. Begin building trust between you and a Part by letting it know what you are able to sense of how it is feeling. For example, Grace said to her Part, "I'm sensing you're feeling a bit wary of me, that you're not sure I will respect your point of view."

If a Part is wary of you, it might have good reason: You might be identified with another Part of you that has an agenda to get this Part to change. If that's happening, you can acknowledge that another Part of you is wanting to change the first Part. You can then make a space for both Parts with *The Power of And.* "I am sensing this Part of me, and I am sensing another Part of me that wants it to change. And I am here with both."

When you are able to acknowledge Parts that have agendas about other Parts without fighting with them or agreeing with them, all your Parts will feel more confident you can meet them where they are. Having said that, even if you offer a Part simple empathy without trying to change it, it probably won't trust you instantly. Trust-building takes time.

Anxious, concerned, worried...

When Grace acknowledged that the Part felt a bit wary of her, she could feel it relax slightly: at least its concerns weren't going to be dismissed outright. Grace could now sense more of what it was feeling. It had a sort of pushing, hurry-up, squeezing quality in her chest. Grace realized this Part felt anxious about something.

Parts are often anxious. For many Parts, their primary motivating emotion is anxiety. They are deeply concerned about you, and whether you will be okay. (Concern is a kind of anxiety. So is worry.) And this makes sense, doesn't it? Parts formed in order to help you with a seriously problematic situation that was too much for you and for those around you to resolve successfully at the time. These Parts know they haven't resolved the situation either. So they are perpetually anxious.

The Part of Grace that constantly pushed her to do more by saying, "You're not enough!" felt anxious.

Listening until it responds "Yes! Exactly! You got it!"

At first, Grace found it hard to maintain Self-in-Presence when a Part of her was telling her, "You're not enough!" She felt a tug toward arguing with it, and coming up with counterexamples. But she realized that arguing with it would be merging with another Part.

You don't need to agree or disagree with what a Part is saying. You are not getting into any kind of a conversation about what it is saying. You are just listening to what it is worried about.

Grace knew that listening with Deep Empathy to the Part that said, "You're not enough!" didn't mean she was going to do what it said or agree with its judgments. Instead she'd be connecting with its intention to be helpful.

We'll use Grace's example to show you how you can increase trust, respect, and relationship with Parts of you that are feeling concerned (or worried or anxious or afraid).

Part Three: The Powers of Presence

1. Grace said to the Part, *"I'm sensing you are worried that I am not enough and I need to do more."*

She then paused and sensed its response. She could tell it felt slightly more understood. Yes, it was worried that Grace was "not enough" and needed to do more.

2. Next, Grace said to the Part, *"Maybe there is something you are not wanting to happen."*

We have found a real difference between saying, "I'm sensing something in me is worried about something" and "I'm sensing something in me doesn't want something to happen."

A note about the wording we are using here: "Maybe there is something you are not wanting to happen" is not a question, but an invitation to sense more deeply. Asking questions of Parts will usually lead you into dead ends. If you ask a Part, "What are you not wanting?" it is likely to reply with all the answers you already know or just not answer at all. So instead, try saying it the way we are showing you.

After Grace said to the Part, "Maybe there is something you are not wanting to happen," she kept her awareness with the Part, without any expectation about what would happen next. What came was a memory of sitting with her quiet, submissive mother at a recent family gathering. She realized this Part didn't want her to be quiet, submissive, and small like her mother. It didn't want her to be controlled by the messages she had received from both the South Korean culture of her home and the wider American culture.

3. Grace then said to the Part, *"I am sensing that you are not wanting me to be quiet, submissive, and small."*

Your job as Self-in-Presence is to get what the Part is Not-wanting. That's all. You are not solving the situation. You are not reassuring the Part that things are going to be okay. You're simply continuing to keep it company, empathically sensing what its worries, concerns, fears and beliefs are about what could happen to you. As you do that, you will gradually sense more and more deeply what this Part is Not-wanting for you.

Going deeper

Grace is already empathizing with her Part when she says to it, "I really get that you are not wanting me to be quiet, submissive, and 'small.'"

The Magic of Empathy

Is there more? Indeed there is. That's why we call this deep empathy. If you just stop after the first couple of responses, there is a tendency to treat this as a problem to be solved in the usual way. But trying to figure out what to do differently would short-circuit the process. In fact, it's what the Parts in your Tangle were already doing—and it hasn't worked.

How do we go deeper? By sensing further into what is not-wanted if that happens.

> 4. Grace said to the Part, *"Maybe there is something you are not-wanting for me **if** I am quiet, submissive, and 'small.'"*

With a sense of surprise, Grace realized something new. *This Part was not wanting her to be Asian!* It heard and came to believe all the messages that being Asian was inferior and wrong.

No wonder all her accomplishments meant nothing to this Part of her! No wonder it was always saying to her, "You are not enough!" None of her accomplishments would ever be enough because none of them would ever stop her from being Asian.

Often, when going deeper with a Tangle, you discover something like this: a Part passionately determined to get you to do something that is literally impossible. It can be a huge relief, as Self-in-Presence, to simply acknowledge that this is what the Part has been trying to get you to do.

Grace realized that not wanting to be Asian was about not wanting all the consequences she had experienced from that—from feeling she should be small and submissive to people making assumptions about her because she was Asian. Even that time in high school, when the boys suddenly found her exotic and desirable, they still weren't seeing past her Asian-ness.

> 5. Grace said to the Part, *"I really get that you are not wanting me to be Asian."*

Tears of compassion welled up in Grace. What an endless, thankless, impossible quest this Part had been on! She let it know she understood how it felt. She said to it, "No wonder you feel that way."

More empathy!

How do we go even deeper from here? By sensing what the Part is not wanting you to *experience* or *feel* if whatever it has said so far happens. A Part's most fundamental dread is that you would have to experience something unbearably awful, something it has been trying all this time to keep you from having to feel.

6. Grace then said to the Part, *"Maybe there is something you are not wanting for me **to experience or feel** from being Asian."*

Notice that as you go deeper, it will take longer for a Part to respond. It is as if it hasn't got a ready answer and needs time to sense for what it is not wanting you to feel.

At this point, you may feel its responses as physical sensations in the central area of your body. Or, as in Grace's case, as something shown to you before you have words for it.

Then, as before, she stayed with the Part and sensed further. Again, she saw her mother: physically tiny, fragile, and diffident, being treated with disdain by her male relatives.

She realized the Part was showing her what it was not wanting her to feel, but it was hard to put into words. Her chest was painfully tight as she searched for the just-right words to capture the essence of that vivid image.

Grace tried out the words "inferior", no... "lesser," no... Long pause. Ah... the Part didn't want her to feel "easily crushed."

A deep breath came. "Easily crushed" fit the image of her mother and the feeling in her body perfectly. These words were new; this feeling had never been articulated before. The tightness in Grace's chest released with a profound sense of relief.

For me or for it?

Perhaps you noticed something subtle about the way Grace was using language in those last few steps of the process.

> *"I really get that you are not wanting me to be Asian. Maybe there is something you are not wanting **for me** to experience or feel from being Asian."*

The invitations were not about what the Part was not wanting *for itself*, but about what it was not wanting *for Grace*.

It's not that Parts don't want anything for themselves. All Parts value being treated with respect and don't want to be ignored, dismissed, or shamed. But when you are listening for their deepest fears and greatest

The Magic of Empathy

hopes, those are for you and not for themselves. Parts are passionately devoted to the well-being of all of you.

When a Part feels heard

What Grace experienced is one of the things that can happen when a Part feels that its Not-wanting has been heard: a satisfying sense of relief radiating through her body. If you experience that sense of relief, take the time to enjoy how that feels in your body now.

Is there always that kind of relief? No. Here's what else could happen:

- You might start to feel in your body the emotions that Part of you has been trying to protect you from experiencing. We will say more about what's probably happening here in Chapter Fifteen, *The Healing Power of Love*.

- You might have a feeling in your body that is vaguely uncomfortable or unclear, doesn't feel particularly emotional, or can't be described easily. Usually there is a sense of something being stuck or frozen. We will address this in detail in Chapter Seventeen, *The Thawing of the Frozen Core*.

- Or what a Part is Wanting for you begins to emerge quite naturally.

Wanting: The other side of dread is desire

All Parts have dread and desire—in other words, they all have something they are Not-wanting and Wanting for you. In fact, dread and desire are as close as not wanting to die is to wanting to live.

What the Part is Not-wanting for you is what it is wanting to protect you from. What the Part is Wanting is what it is not wanting you to miss out on or fail to experience.

A Part might express what it wants for you by saying it as something it doesn't want. A Part might say, "I'm not wanting you to miss the chance to live a fulfilling life," and you could say back, "Ah! You are *wanting* for me to live a fulfilling life!"

A Part might have been telling you all the things it's not wanting you to experience, and right in the middle of all of that, it starts saying, "I want you to be able to …" You could reply to it: "Oh, you are wanting me to be able to …"

A Part might let you know it has a specific desire. Just acknowledge whatever that desire is. Remember that the impulse to rush out and try to get whatever that Part is asking for comes from another Part. Fulfilling a Part's request is not included in being empathic to it. Just say to it: "I can sense how much you want *that* for me."

There are emotions that are already kinds of Wanting: wishing, hoping, craving, needing, demanding. Even feeling frustrated is a kind of Wanting. After all, when you're frustrated, there's something you want that you're not getting, or something you want to do, but you can't. So if you can sense that a Part is feeling one of these emotions, you are already beginning to sense what it is Wanting.

Wanting can connect you with the life energy trapped in a Tangle. But to do that we need to go below the surface.

Going deeper with Wanting

Let's return to Grace's story to illustrate going deeper with Wanting. After Grace heard that the Part that had been pushing her to do more was not wanting her to feel easily crushed, she felt a profound sense of relief. At that point, it felt like a good time to sense for what this Part was Wanting for her.

Here is the sequence of steps that Grace went through:

1. Grace said to the Part, *"Maybe you are wanting something for me."*

Taking time, Grace sensed that this Part wanted her to be free to be herself regardless of what others thought and regardless of how she looked.

"I really hear that what you want for me is to be free to be myself regardless of what others think and regardless of how I look."

She paused, patiently, to let that much sink in before moving to the next step. Then Grace went on to sense what that Part wanted her to *experience from having that*. As before, this empathic invitation was carefully phrased.

2. She said to the Part, *"Maybe there is something you are wanting for me to experience* **if** *I am able to be free to be myself."*

Grace knew that asking a question would be likely to short-circuit the process by implying that an answer should come quickly. In fact, at these deeper stages of empathy, the Part needs time for it to be able to respond.

The Magic of Empathy

After a couple of minutes of silently sensing in her body, what came to her was that the Part wanted her to experience *confident self-love*. That was new! She couldn't recall ever saying that before. And yet it felt absolutely right. There was an undeniable sense of rightness to the words "confident self-love." Grace took her time to fully receive how right they felt.

Was there more to the process? Indeed there was. Grace had learned that you can keep going, sensing more and more deeply what a Part is wanting for you until you experience an essential quality of aliveness in your body right now.

3. Grace said to the Part, *"I really get that you want me to experience confident self-love... and maybe there is something you **want me to be able to feel** from experiencing that."*

After a while, Grace began to feel her skin tingling pleasantly. She had a delightful sense of lightness and flexibility throughout her body. This was what this Part wanted for her *to be able to feel* from experiencing confident self-love.

What often comes at this point is something felt throughout your whole body. Fresh language, images, metaphors are needed to capture that kind of experience: "It feels like sitting by the fireplace with a cat on my lap," or "It's like Champagne bubbles drifting up through my body." Or it may be an enjoyable feeling that has no words at all, as Grace experienced.

At this point, Grace was no longer aware of a separate Part of her revealing its Wanting. She was able to simply savor, soak in, revel in, and fully feel the lightness, flexibility, and tingling all over her skin.

It felt wonderful. It was her own precious aliveness.

The Power of Deep Empathy

1. Take time to sense which Part needs your attention first.

2. Sense how that Part is feeling—what its emotion is—and let it know you can sense that.

3. If it is feeling anxious, sad, angry or afraid, you can invite it to let you know what it is not wanting to happen to you.

   - And when you sense its response, let it know you hear

it/sense it/get it.

- Continue to sense what it is not wanting *if that* happens until there is a sense of relief.

4. If it is wishing, hoping, craving, needing, demanding something or feeling frustrated about something, invite it to let you know what it is wanting for you if it gets what it wants.

- Continue to invite it to let you know what it is wanting for you to feel or experience *if that* happens until you can feel a sense of aliveness in your body.

5. Take time to feel any positive feelings in your body.

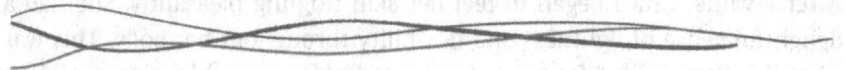

It's all about relationship

When you are sensing what a Part is dreading or desiring for you, the answers you get are not as important as the relationship you are cultivating. You're not going down a checklist to get to the next bit of information. The quality of your relationship with the Part is what makes it possible for a Part to trust you.

When you do this work, you need to take your time. We can't emphasize this enough. None of this will work if it is done in a hurry, or when you're merged with a Part that is impatient, or if you try to guess what the answer is instead of waiting to let it come. Pause... sense... take your time.

A Tangle doesn't untangle in just one session. The time you take to build a trusting inner relationship will be well worth it. You might need to continue to develop your relationship with this Part over several sessions before it is able to trust you and reveal its deepest dreads and dearest hopes.

There is more to the Untangling process than just *The Power of Deep Empathy*, yet this one important Power can be transformative in itself. It's as if your inner compass has been handed back to you. The right direction for your life becomes obvious. Possibilities emerge that simply didn't exist in the known universe when all you felt was anxious and confused about what to do.

Over and over we have found that when a Part feels it has been fully heard, something quite remarkable happens. The Part's opposition to other Parts fades away, and its strengths and abilities become your strengths and abilities. And you might even find that, despite everything, the truth is that you are already profoundly, fundamentally okay.

No matter what their superficial strategies are, Parts are driven by what they dread and desire for you. When their fears and longings are heard within a trusting relationship, Parts transform—and Tangles release.

Part Three: The Powers of Presence

Chapter 14
A TALE OF TWO PARTS

Now that you are learning how important Deep Empathy is for untangling your Tangles, it is time for us to reveal something important about Parts.

It's this: The Parts you encounter at the surface of your Tangle are always of two main types. And those two types of Parts appreciate being treated in different ways.

We didn't always know this. When we began Untangling, the first Parts we were aware of were Ann's Part that drank, Barbara's Part that ate, Ann's Part that refused to write, and Barbara's Part that went back to bed and pulled the covers over its head.

All this type of Part seemed to care about was getting what it wanted. Now! If it wanted to drink, it drank. If it wanted to eat, it ate. If it wanted to sleep, it slept. It didn't care what other people thought. It wasn't concerned about the long-term consequences of its actions. It wanted what it wanted, when it wanted it, and that was that.

After we had been working with Parts for about a year, we realized there was another type of Part operating in our Tangles. It was the Part of Ann that tried to get her to stop drinking. It was the Part of Barbara that was horrified when she reached for more food and cheered when she restrained herself. It scolded Ann when she got to the end of the day without doing any writing. It made Barbara feel she was such a useless waste of space that she might as well die.

Imagine a car driven by a reckless and impulsive child. The car is careening along the road, barely missing disaster after disaster. A terrified older child is stuck in the passenger seat, unable to do anything but shout, "Don't go so fast! Slow down! Where are you going? Don't go on the highway! Oh no, you idiot!" But nothing it says can stop the devil-may-care driver.

Of our two types of Parts, one Part is like the kid behind the wheel of the car. It can take action in the world—it can drive. Another type of Part can

Part Three: The Powers of Presence

only tell the driver what to do. It tries to control through admonitions, advice, and being judgmental. The situation is more nuanced than that, true, but in essence that is what these two different kinds of Parts are like.

These two types of Parts, so different in character and capabilities, can be found in every Tangle. *You* aren't either of those Parts.

When you are Self-in-Presence, you are able to be the space where any and all your Parts can be the way they are, and your actions are based on what you value and what fits the situation instead of being pushed around by your Parts.

The Driver

Let's start with the Part that climbs into the driver's seat. We call it a *Defender*. Barbara's Part that ate and read and slept is this type of Part. Ann's Part that avoided writing was also a Defender, as was Ann's Part that drank.

We already told you a lot about Defenders in Chapter Four, *Hijack* and Chapter Six, *Rebellion*. We just hadn't referred to them as Defenders yet.

Defenders can act—or refuse to act—and they don't have to have a long-drawn-out conversation with anyone in order to do so. They can just act. They are responsible for most of the actions you take inside a Tangle.

Sometimes the actions a Defender takes can be uncomfortable and involve a lot of effort. Barbara had a Part that craved Dick Francis novels, and she would find herself out in the pouring rain wandering around the streets of London for hours trying to locate another one as soon as she had finished the last one.

Sometimes the actions it takes will be almost unconscious. Ann's Part would be out the door, taking her to the liquor store, right on time to get her evening bottle of wine without any apparent planning or thought.

This type of Part can be remarkably adept in putting off or avoiding doing anything it doesn't want to do. Ann's Defenders would conveniently forget about making an important phone call or having that difficult conversation or getting to bed on time.

Barbara would find herself doing something that was clearly *extremely* important like carefully tidying the stack of books by her bed, then wind up reading until it was simply too late to do whatever was on her task list for that day.

Recognizing when a Defender has the car keys

It can be surprisingly difficult to recognize a Defender. At first it often seems to be you who is surfing the internet or working super-hard until way past knocking-off time. Their feelings of upset or sadness or anger may feel like your feelings.

There are some qualities you can look for that can help you to recognize when this kind of Part is active in your life. They live almost entirely in the present, concerned with only the immediate future. They act automatically, impulsively, and compulsively, with little or no regard to any possible negative consequences of their behavior. And, as we have said, they don't have to consult with anyone before they do whatever it is they want to do.

When you are in the grip of a Defender it can feel that your will and body have been taken over. So when you feel you don't have control of what you're doing, it's likely that a Defender has grabbed the car keys.

Here is a list of clues that can help you spot when a Defender is doing the driving. You may not experience all of these, but you will experience at least one of them when a Defender is behind the wheel.

Signs you are merged with a Defender

- You feel grumpy, cranky, resentful, upset, teary, rebellious—even when the situation doesn't warrant that kind of response.
- You do things you know are "bad" for you but you just can't stop.
- You don't do things you want to do or know you should do—at least not without great reluctance and difficulty.
- You feel swamped, overwhelmed and swept away by your emotions.

It is usually fairly easy to feel in your body how a Defender is feeling. You may sense its emotions: anger, sadness, confusion, longing. You may be aware of physical discomfort, often in the middle of your body: something heavy pressing on your chest, an ache around your heart, or a pain in your belly.

The Passenger

In a Tangle the second type of Part is in the position of a helpless passenger. We call it a *Protector*. Chapter Five, *Takeover*, and Chapter Seven, *Intimidation*, were primarily about Protectors.

Part Three: The Powers of Presence

It was a revelation to us when we realized there was a type of Part that couldn't act in the world. But then it made sense: Why would it be telling us what to do if it could do it itself? It would just do it, right?

Think how scary and frustrating it would be being driven around by an emotional, impulsive child. Since there's not much you can do to directly affect the course and speed of the car, you're left with your powers of persuasion—including giving advice, manipulating, criticizing, and shaming.

No wonder this kind of Part is so anxious and gets so frustrated.

Recognizing when a Protector is trying to take over

Protectors are overwhelmingly concerned for your safety—whatever that means to them. They worry almost incessantly: "What will happen?" "What will other people think?" "What's going to go wrong?"

Protectors are like security officers with banks of monitors. They track what's going on. They watch what you do and think and feel. They set off alarms when something happens they feel is unsafe.

Because Protectors are so worried and deeply frustrated, they often behave like stressed-out parents: scolding, controlling, advising, blocking, pushing, encouraging, or frantically warning you. Of course, they are not really parents. They can seem parent-like because they may have learned their language and methods from your parents or other caregivers. They have that parental quality of extreme concern without power to effect change.

Protectors spend a lot of time and energy trying to analyze what the problem is and figure out what you should do about it. They can be brilliant at it! If the problem were just an ordinary, non-tangled one, that approach would probably work. But, unfortunately, inside a Tangle, it is wasted effort.

Carrots and sticks

As we have said, to make something happen, a Protector has to get another Part of you to do it. Since Protectors must influence other Parts, they have developed a whole host of strategies for doing so.

Protectors can create visions of the delights awaiting you if you do what they tell you: "You will look so gorgeous when you can fit into that size four dress," "If you read these books on relationships you will find and keep the perfect partner who totally loves and understands you," "If you work super-hard and get your manager to see how amazing you are, you will soar high in the company."

Since a Protector thinks that you are the Part it is trying to influence, it says "you." But it's really talking to another Part, which is usually a Defender.

Protectors can try to scare you with dire consequences if you don't listen to them: "You'll wind up homeless, penniless, and living out of garbage bags!" or "You're never going to get a boy/girlfriend if you keep on eating like that."

They can be subtle and manipulative, as in: "Don't you think you could try a little harder?" They can even sound helpful, making suggestions about what you could do: "Just think positive!" "Make a plan and stick to it!" "You'd better find a coach."

And, of course, they can use criticism in all the varieties that you know so well to prod you into doing what they believe will make you happy and safe.

Slamming on the brakes

Often Protectors want to stop you from doing something. They can lecture you about what you should stop doing and parade before you all the terrible things that will happen if you persist, but this is not always entirely successful with a strongly motivated Defender.

Protectors have another trick up their sleeve to try to stop you from doing something. They can act on your body. They can:

- restrict your breathing by constricting your throat or chest
- give you headaches and stomachaches
- make you overwhelmingly tired
- distort your sight

Yes, that's right. Protectors can't act in the world, but they *can* act on your body. It's as if the passenger grabs the driver by the neck. Not very safe, but hey, it might work to stop what the Protector sees as the car's headlong rush to destruction.

Some signs of a Protector

Protectors can seem to be your thoughts, your ego, your conscience, an "inner critic" or what you think other people would say. For example:

Part Three: The Powers of Presence

- You feel what you're doing is never enough.
- You feel like you have to figure out, solve, and take care of everything, or doom will fall.
- You find yourself saying, "I should," "I must," "I have to."
- You compare yourself to other people—and you are always coming up short.
- You say to yourself: "You're just lazy," "You're pathetic."
- You feel sure you are going to be found out as a bad person or a fraud.
- You lie awake in the dark unable to stop your thoughts from anxiously chasing themselves around in circles.

They come in pairs

These two types of Parts, Defenders and Protectors, almost always appear together. This is because they react to each other.

A Defender that stubbornly refuses to do something can trigger an attack by a Protector. The Protector might try to push the Defender into doing what it wants by contemptuously shaming it into good behavior.

A Protector might try to control a Defender by tightly squeezing the chest or constricting the throat, making it hard to breathe or speak. This can trigger the reaction of a Defender that objects to feeling painfully confined. It might try to fight back against being restricted, or it might simply collapse under the pressure.

Although they often occur together, you can't always tell that two Parts are present. You're likely to be identified with one of them and struggling with the other. If you hear yourself saying something like, "No matter how hard I try, I can't seem to get that greedy, self-indulgent Part of me to stop eating gigantic bowls of buttered popcorn whenever it's depressed," you're identified with a Protector trying to control and manage what seems to be an out-of-control, misbehaving Part of you. *The Power of And* will help you acknowledge both Parts: the Part that eats buttered popcorn when depressed, *and* the Part trying to control it.

If you feel like a rebellious teenager who's flipping the bird to all authority figures, both inner and outer, you're probably identified with a Defender.

Likewise if you feel small, downtrodden, crushed under the weight of expectation and inner demands. It's time to acknowledge both Parts with *The Power of And,* the one that is rebelling or collapsing under harsh treatment, and the one that is trying to manage, manipulate, or control the first one.

The importance of the right kind of relationship

Protectors and Defenders need different kinds of attention, just as children of different ages need you to be with them in different ways.

Defenders are highly attuned to the quality of their relationship with you. If you think you're dealing with a Defender, you'll probably want to spend some time just sensing how it feels in your body. Next you'll need to sense what kind of company or contact it would like from you right now.

Protectors appreciate having their concerns treated with respect. If you think you're dealing with a Protector, your ideal first approach will be something like, "Hello! I'm wondering if you are concerned about something."

The kind of relationship Defenders respond to

Defenders have mainly had to deal with Protectors who try to control them, so they can be extremely sensitive about how they are being treated. They can become reactive and angry or withdraw altogether if criticized or pushed, even indirectly.

A Defender doesn't yet know *you*. It often takes time for a Defender to trust your motives for wanting to get to know it. Are you going to try to get it to do something? Are you going to make demands of it? Are you going to try to make it change?

Because Defenders can mistrust you initially, it's important to pay attention to the quality of your relationship with them. We recommend saying something like, "I'm wondering how you would like me to be with you right now." Rather than hearing a verbal response, you're likely to see or feel the Defender's response: "It wants me to back off and not get too close" or "It wants me to go slowly and give it time." You might also get a warmer reaction, such as: "It's climbing into my lap and wants a cuddle."

It can be revolutionary for a Defender to be with someone who simply keeps it company just the way it is, with no pressure to do anything and no pressure to change how it is.

Part Three: The Powers of Presence

Here is some language that can help as you spend time with a Defender:

- "I am here with you, just the way you are."
- "I am wondering how you would like me to be with you right now."
- "It's okay if you don't trust me."
- "Take all the time you need."

The kind of relationship Protectors respond to

Protectors are often on the edge of flat-out panic. Nonetheless, they are usually open to letting you know what they are concerned about when you approach them with interest and respect.

Protectors want their concerns to be heard and respected. Initially, that is what's most important to them. They are generally not looking for tenderness or sympathy, or hugs and cuddles, especially when you first get to know them.

They have an exhausting job to do, one they have always believed they were alone in doing. Protectors often want to be appreciated for the hard work they have done and for how long they have done it. As they slowly come to believe they are not alone, they will start to relax and trust you.

In Chapter Thirteen, *The Magic of Empathy,* we showed you how to empathize with a Protector's concerns without getting caught up in whether their beliefs are valid or whether the actions they advocate are wise. Protectors are often especially helped by listening attentively to what they are Not-wanting and Wanting. Here is some language that can help:

- "It sounds like you might be worried about something."
- "I'm here to listen, if you'd like to tell me what you're worried about."
- "Maybe there is something you are not wanting to happen to me."
- "I *really* get how hard you've been working to help me."

Do you need to know what type of Part it is?

As you have seen, Defenders and Protectors are different in several ways. They have different challenges and issues. They want to be related to differently. Being sensitive to a Part's needs will help you develop your relationship with it so that it can turn to you with confidence and trust. That's why it can help to know what kind of Part you are with.

Having said that, we urge you not to stress about what type of Part it is. If you're not sure, it's probably not clear yet. Parts may reveal themselves slowly, often showing more about themselves as your relationship with them deepens. It's often through a Part's interactions with you and with other Parts in your Tangle that it becomes obvious what type of Part it is. The most important thing is to be curious, empathic and patient.

Once a Defender realizes and starts to trust that you are not the controlling, judgmental Part it feels resentful toward, it is glad. It has actually been waiting for you. You can supply the relationship it needs.

Once a Protector realizes and starts to trust that you are not the emotional, impulsive Part that it is worried about, it is glad. Like a child home alone, the Protector is grateful when a real adult finally shows up. It can lay down its lonely burden once it knows that you are there.

There is another important process that often happens when Defenders and Protectors start to calm down, relax, and trust you. A third type of Part can emerge into your awareness, one that is close to the core of the Tangle. We call it a *Small One*.

A Small One is a special kind of Defender

A few years after we began developing Untangling, we noticed something interesting about Defenders. They weren't only defending themselves. They also seemed to be defending another Part that felt younger, more vulnerable, less verbal.

It was often so close to the Defender that the two of them seemed as if they were one Part. But with time and caring attention, what appeared to be a single part separated into two: The Defender that we were already aware of, and another more hidden Part.

Your Tangle originated when something in your life was impossible. You had feelings about that whole impossible situation: distress, shock, fear, anger, grief, helplessness, and so on but those feelings had no way to be felt and moved on from. The whole experience got stuck in a kind of limbo. The Part that has continued to carry those unchanged feelings we call the Small One.

Part Three: The Powers of Presence

When you first meet it, a Small One is an odd, not yet fully formed, halfway-here kind of experience. Here are some examples of what a Small One might be like when you first make contact with it:

- an uncomfortable wordless feeling in the middle of your body
- something in you that feels raw, fragile, tender, or "needy"
- something hiding or hidden (in a cave, behind a door, under a blanket, in a box, in a shell...)
- something in you that seems inanimate, like a stone

Small Ones have many of the qualities of Defenders. Most importantly, they can act. Their actions are motivated by the need to fill in something which has been missing. Chapter Nine, *Longing*, was about one of the primary activities of Small Ones: pursuing love and devotion in a single-minded way.

As for the kind of relationship that Small Ones respond to—well, we need a whole chapter to tell you about that. The next one.

Chapter 15
THE HEALING POWER OF LOVE

ANN: I'd already spent time with many Parts in my most tangled Tangle, and I still wasn't free of it. I still kept falling into "fascination" with a certain kind of man, one who was perceptive and empathic but who was also emotionally unavailable. I'd think about him far too much, and definitely couldn't have a genuine human-to-human relationship with him. And because I was hiding most of what was going on for me, I couldn't have genuine relationships with anyone else, either. I felt frustrated, ashamed, tired of it all—but unable to stop.

Barbara reminded me that I hadn't yet been in contact with the Small One in this Tangle, so I sat down with the intention to invite and spend time with this Small One.

At first, I was aware of nothing. All I could sense was a profound blankness.

Then I began to feel that this blankness was somewhere deep down, like the floor of a cellar. A dirt floor. I waited, sensing.

I started to feel like there was someone there. Invisible? Hiding? I didn't know. I waited.

Then, slowly, the dirt of the cellar floor began to rise. Two eyes appeared. Just two eyes, not a person or an animal. Someone was there—and it was enough for us to begin to have a relationship. I could begin to get to know what this Part of me, this Small One, was feeling.

The primary thing it was feeling, at first, was that it didn't trust me. I needed to earn its trust. And the only way to do that, clearly, was simply to be there with it, accepting it just as it was.

How do you reach out to develop a trusting relationship with something only partly there? Answer: Extremely gently and super slowly. This kind of relationship starts with intention: "I want you to feel safe with me." And it includes permission: "Take your time. There's no rush. I'm here when you're ready."

Think of a rescue dog brought home with a history of hard times. It crawls under the porch and refuses to come out. You can hardly even see it cowering back there in the shadows—but you know it's there. Trying to grab hold of it will just make it draw back even more (or make it attack you). So you sit down somewhere. You notice how close you can get before it starts to feel anxious and you move back a bit but you also don't go away. You wait. You want it to be able to feel safe with you. If you give it calm, patient company it will be able to relax and eventually it will move toward you. The first step in your relationship is sensing what will help it to be comfortable and relaxed in your company.

It's a good thing that, as Self-in-Presence, you have qualities of patience and steadiness that you can draw on, because you will need them. Winning the trust of a Small One takes time.

What happens next

A stronger sense of this younger Part of you will develop. Even before it starts to feel like somebody, it will probably start to feel like something. As you stay with it, you'll feel it more and more clearly. Notice what it is like and where you feel it in your body. It is usually, but not always, in your stomach and abdomen area. All you need to do is rest your awareness with it.

Other Parts of you will almost undoubtedly spring into action to try to soothe or numb or shut down these feelings. Defender Parts will try to distract and soothe you by using their go-to hijacking strategies. Protector Parts may use harsh names ("defective," "broken," "pitiful") or show you repellent images to scare you away from it (a dead baby, a writhing pit of snakes, being covered in scuttling bugs).

If Parts like that appear, you'll turn toward them, acknowledge them, and spend time hearing what they are worried about, as in Chapter Thirteen, The Magic of Empathy. (In Chapter Sixteen, Last-Ditch Efforts, we'll say more about why such Parts are likely to appear as you get close to a Small One.) After receiving some empathy for their concerns, these Parts are likely to calm down. You'll then be able to bring your attention back to how the Small One feels in your body.

The Healing Power of Love

At this point, to deepen your accepting relationship with this younger Part of you, you can take time to sense precisely what it feels like physically. You can notice where you are aware of those feelings in your body without trying to do anything to them. You don't ask the Part anything. You don't try to change it. You simply give attention to what it is already showing you: what it feels like right now.

ANN: I could feel that someone was there, and it was not sure if it could trust me. I let it know it could take all the time it needed... and then I began to feel it in my body.

It was tight, like "gripping," in my stomach and abdomen area. I felt it more on the left than the right. I didn't have to understand why it felt this way; it just did.

As you spend more time with it, and it starts to trust that you are not going to do anything to it, you'll start to be able to feel more of its emotions. Because you experience its feelings in your own body, you will know firsthand its longing, its terror, its rage, its helplessness.

These feelings may even be strong and uncomfortable, but as Self-in-Presence, you know you are still okay. In fact, it can be a relief to feel what this Part of you has been needing to feel for a long time. You can be there with this Part and its feelings, however they are, subtle or strong.

ANN: The longer I stayed with how this Small One felt in my body, the more I could feel its emotions. It was howling with helplessness, longing to be free, and despairing that it ever would be. I felt how it felt in my body, and I let it know I felt it.

Giving this kind of simple attention might not seem like much, but in fact it is the most important and transformational thing you can do. As we said in Chapter Nine, Longing, it is the quality of caring attention that was missing when the Tangle first formed that is most needed from you now.

Memories or metaphors?

As you stay with the Small One, images may come. These might be memories from your childhood, or young adulthood—really from any time earlier than now. Or they might be clearly metaphorical. Barbara had a vivid image of her arms being cut off that captured how powerless something in her felt. Our friend Valerie had a Part that showed her an animal's leg in a trap, getting more and more mangled as the animal tried to pull free.

Or what a Small One shows you may seem to be memories. Barbara clearly remembers being marched upstairs by her unforgiving father and him pulling out his gardening gloves and spanking her until her mother asked if that was enough yet.

But sometimes it's not clear if the images that come are memories or if they are metaphors. What it shows you may or may not have happened. Trying to determine the literal truth of what you are being shown at this stage will hold back the process.

What's important is that this Part is expressing what it was like for it to go through what did happen. What matters is that you keep it company, lovingly, compassionately. This is its reality and needs to be respected as such.

ANN: The Small One felt like it was locked in a small, dark, enclosed space, able to see out but unable to move. I didn't know if this had ever actually happened to me—and I knew I didn't need to try to find out. What mattered was that for the Small One, it was really happening, and it was happening right now.

Past and present are one and the same for a Small One

In a Tangle, past and present become mixed together. What is now and what was then become confused. In a very real way, for the Small One, the past is eternally now.

It's not so much that the feelings have been there just waiting to be felt. It's more that they have never had a chance to form enough for you to be able to feel them. Feeling these unformed and unfelt feelings is what has been waiting to happen.

We are not saying you have to feel the feelings in exactly the way you would have felt them at the time. In fact, plunging into the center of painful feelings as if they were happening to you now doesn't help and can even make things worse. What does help is to be Self-in-Presence as you feel the feelings as they come now, in this present moment.

ANN: I let the Small One know I could feel what it was going through, being trapped in a dark enclosed space, feeling helpless and despairing. I said to it, "I get how hard that is for you. It was that hard—and still is."

As your grown-up self, you know that you have already lived through whatever happened originally. It isn't happening now. You are no longer the younger you who went through all that. You have many more resources than you had then. As Self-in-Presence, you can be with the Part of you who is now able to have those feelings as you are experiencing them directly in your body. When a Small One can receive your present-time acceptance and love, you will finally be able to experience what happened back then in a way that can resolve and move forward.

Being with a Small One

One of Barbara's favorite metaphors for a way of being with a Small One is sitting or crouching down beside it with absolutely no intention of going anywhere or doing anything. She may spend many minutes simply sensing how her body feels as she keeps her attention with this Part of her, noticing exactly where she feels something and what it is like.

At some point she will start to have some kind of knowing about how it is for that Part to be in the world right now. Then she will let it know she can sense that. It is a finely-tuned combination of feeling how it feels in her body and empathic company with that younger Part of her.

For Ann, the Small One is often like an image that is somehow connected to something she is feeling in her body. One time she experienced a Small One as like a patch of tar on the road, located to the left of her midsection.

Sometimes other Parts of her wonder if spending time with something like this has any value at all. When this happens, she acknowledges them as well. She likes to remind herself, "I'm not doing anything, I'm not going anywhere, I'm just being here."

If it's showing you how painful something feels to it, you'll say to it, "I get how hard that was for you. It was that hard—and still is." Sometimes at this point we need a double verb, combining both past and present in one: "I get how hard that is/was for you."

What a Small One needs from you is no more (and no less) than simply this: sensing and describing precisely how it feels in your body and being with it in the way it needs you to be.

Your body is where feelings are experienced. As you keep a younger Part company, you can sense its feelings in your body and describe them. Go slowly. Bring your awareness to precisely where they are in your body. Sense what they are like. Allow the descriptions to emerge. Take time to check those descriptions and revise them until they accurately fit what you are sensing.

Sometimes what is needed for this process to complete itself now is not only to describe but also to express the emotions that were frozen before they could be felt and expressed at the time. When emotions are frozen, you can feel how the flow of energy in your body gets stopped.

When the emotions of a younger Part are expressed, you can feel energy flowing freely through your body again. Even when the emotions are painful, there is a feeling of relief that this is finally being known and expressed.

"You can be this way for as long as you need to be"

As Self-in-Presence, you do not need to know if the Small One's feelings will ever change. All you need to know is that the Small One needs you to be with it exactly as it is.

You need to be present with a Small One that is suffering without trying to help it feel better, even though this can be challenging to other Parts of you. A Protector Part may appear, worrying that these feelings will never change. A Defender may try to hijack you by sweeping you away into floods of emotion or distracting behaviors.

By now you know how to give compassionate company to Protectors and Defenders and then turn back to the Small One.

It can be important to say to the Small One, "You can be the way you are for as long as you need to be." Barbara had a Small One that felt life was so painful it just wanted to find a way to escape. The only thing that brought it relief was to say to it, "I really sense how painful and difficult life feels for you. I can sense how you feel you'd just like to crawl into a hole and give up. I am here, and you can be the way you are for as long as you need to be."

You might be deeply touched by what a Small One is showing you. Tears of compassion may come to your eyes. There can be a deep and heartfelt connection, which is felt by both you and the Small One. When you are absorbed in being with a Small One, there can be a timeless quality, as if both of you are soaking up the sweetness of this contact.

Some challenges being with a Small One

Just as a rescue dog might snap at your hand before it comes to trust you, a Small One might challenge you in a number of ways, especially when you are first getting to know it.

When a Small One makes demands

What if, for example, a Small One asks you to fix how things are or demands that you keep it safe forever? Our student Jameel told us about a Small One who said to him accusingly, "Why aren't you helping me?" He felt guilty and under pressure to do something for his suffering Small One. Then he realized he'd gotten merged with another Part of him.

We recommended he say this: "I really hear how you would so much like this situation to be made better, and you would like me or someone to do that for you. Of course! That makes so much sense. And how it is now is really hard for you. I can really sense that."

It's not a good idea to say, "I will always be here to protect you from harm," or "Everything is going to be all right." Parts are sensitive to truth. Their trust in you will diminish if you make promises, because they know that no one can be sure what will happen in the future.

What we recommend for Small Ones in general is also exactly what is needed here: to let this Small One know that you get how hard it is/was (what it is going through), and repeat that you are here with it. You can say, "I can sense how much you want to be protected from harm and I am here with you now."

When a Small One blames you

A Small One may blame you or others and demand, "Why haven't you protected me?" You may genuinely regret you that were not able to protect it. You can let it know that you get how much it wanted to be protected. You can say, "I know how much you wish I had protected you. I wasn't always there for you and that was hard for you. I wish I could have been. I really hear how hard that is and was for you. I am here now."

When you are not enough for a Small One

What if a Small One says to you that you are not enough for it? It might let you know that it wants someone reliable to care for it, and it doesn't believe that you are capable of that. Your response is simply this: "I am here with you now, and I really hear how much you are longing for someone else to care for you."

It's important to remember that you as Self-in-Presence do not have to give a younger Part everything it feels it needs. Your job is to be present to it with empathy. And in fact, although it may not know this, your being empathically present is what it most needs in order to heal and rejoin your wholeness.

A Small One transforms

A Small One can completely transform in the twinkling of an eye. Here is the kind of thing we hear people say: "I thought it was a wounded, weak, fragile part of me, but I discovered it's full of life. Irrepressible life!" "I thought it was just an ugly, disgusting part of me but when I actually felt it, it was glowing and beautiful and alive."

This change is often non-linear. It can go from feeling that this is simply how it is and it's going to be like this forever to suddenly becoming quite different. A Part that seems to be like a patch of tar can morph into being a baby chick in the blink of an eye. A little child can grow up into a fully grown adult in the space of a few breaths. Although this transformation happens surprisingly quickly, it usually comes after an extended period of deep, patient, caring contact.

ANN: After a long time of simply being with the Small One in the way it needed, feeling how it felt and letting it know I was with it, suddenly I found myself in an open field. The feelings in my body had utterly transformed from being unable to move in a small, enclosed space into an experience of vivid spacious aliveness. I wasn't aware any longer of a Small One separate from me. I was all there, eager to explore this new world.

Such transformations have to be experienced to be believed, but we have both seen them so many times, we are not surprised when they happen. Not surprised... yet always awestruck, to see life itself emerging from what had been so dark and confined.

As this process continues, Small Ones and other Parts dissolve, and all their life-enhancing energy, attributes and abilities become you. This transformation allows you to be who you truly are: capable of being present in the situations and interactions of your life without being overshadowed by your past. Your past is still your past. But it does not destroy you or define you. Even the worst of it is something you now own—on your terms. No one can take that away from you. And everything you have learned and developed in the time since this younger Part formed, you get to keep as well.

When a Small One becomes you, your essential qualities of Self-in-Presence are strengthened:

- Your autonomy
- Your authenticity
- Your capacity to interact freely
- Your clarity
- Your ability to be assertive when needed
- Your spontaneity
- Your playfulness
- Your strength
- Your ability to love—and receive love

In all of these ways and more, the transformation of a Small One means that you are more fully alive right here and right now.

Part Three: The Powers of Presence

Chapter 16
LAST-DITCH EFFORTS

Remember what it is like when there's an emergency on the Starship Enterprise? Whooping alarms. Big solid fire-doors slamming shut. Kirk commanding Scotty to divert all power to the shields. Spock striding to his science station with a frown on his Vulcan face. Captain and crew all mobilized for ultimate protection and safety.

When a threat is sensed, defenses are activated. That's only natural—and it's that way in a Tangle, too. When it feels like the threat could destroy the very essence of who you are, Defenders and Protectors put out their maximum, last-ditch efforts to try to stop what they believe endangers you. They'll fight on, using *anything* they hope will save you, all the way to the last ditch.

Don't go there!

As you cultivate Self-in-Presence and spend time with your Parts, you will get closer and closer to directly experiencing the core of your Tangle. As that happens, your Protectors and Defenders believe you are getting way too close to something life-threateningly dangerous. They believe that if you experience it, you will not be able to handle it. You might go crazy! You might have a breakdown! Or even worse.

Whenever your Tangle first developed, you may have been too young, or too hurt, or too unsupported to be able to experience how that felt at the time. It might well have been genuinely unbearable with the limited resources you had then. Without the resources you needed, keeping it in a deep freeze made perfect sense.

Your Defenders and Protectors developed lots of strategies to keep you away from this experience that, even now, they're sure would be impossible for you to bear. After all, how would they know you've matured and gained new resources and developed new abilities?

Their strategies have been tried and tested, honed and perfected over many years. And they become exceedingly worried when they feel their strategies are being undermined or challenged. For them, the danger is real. For them, this is a happening-right-now-life-and-death emergency that needs them to use their most extreme defenses.

So they often up their game when they're afraid you're getting too close to something they've been protecting, bringing in the "big guns" as they deploy their last-ditch attempts to keep you away from the core of your Tangle.

A Protector's last-ditch efforts

Protectors panic as your awareness gets closer to the core of your Tangle. They'll use whatever means they deem necessary to stop you in your tracks.

Remember, Protectors aren't doing any of these things to try to hurt you. They genuinely believe that experiencing the feelings locked up at the heart of your Tangle could destroy you, your life, and possibly even your loved ones. They are protecting you the best way they know.

Here are a few of the common ways Protectors try to keep you safe.

"I can't think!"

One of a Protector's strategies is to make it impossible for you to know what you are experiencing. A Protector can do this by suffusing your consciousness with a mental fog.

They can knock you out by putting you to sleep at a key moment in either an Untangling session or in your life. Your eyelids droop and suddenly your chin is on your chest. After all, if you can't focus on anything, you won't be able to focus on something that Part of you considers dangerous.

"I can hardly breathe!"

As we have said, although Protectors aren't able to take direct action in the world, they can act on your body. When they want you to stop getting closer to something in you, one of their common strategies is constricting your body.

When Protectors panic, these constrictions can get extremely strong, to the point where it can feel like you are being clamped in a vise. You may feel like you are being choked or like you have a tight band around your chest or stomach. You might even get dizzy and feel like you are about to faint.

When you stop doing what you were doing, the Protector will relax a bit and the tension in your body will ease. But if you start paying attention again to whatever it was, the Protector will clamp down on you again.

"It looks horrible!"

As another way of keeping you away from "that down there," Protectors can show you scary images, like spiders, monsters, dead babies... whatever you fear most. One woman said, "I got to a deep place... and there are snakes down there! I hate snakes!" No wonder she stopped going any further.

Protectors know exactly what you are scared of—after all, they are part of you. So they use that knowledge to craft images that will have the greatest stopping power. They create these scary images to enforce their protection.

A person in one of our workshops told us that as she approached a Small One, a Protector warned her: "It will shock you." The Small One then appeared as a "skeleton baby wrapped in a black blanket," which did shock (something in) her... and then a Protector said in a snarky tone, "See if you can love that!"

Protectors can also show you "disaster movies" to stop you from going further. Barbara used to have a very active Protector that would run reel after reel of her beloved daughter being killed in a car crash or murdered or dying of some horrible disease—every time she got closer to something deeper in her Untangling sessions.

This type of Protector doesn't have to speak. It is invisible. It just shows you scary images. When you start imagining scary things, you can guess that a worried Protector is trying to stop you going further.

"This will never work."

Another tactic desperate Protectors use is to say things like:

- "There's nothing there!"
- "This personal growth stuff doesn't work."
- "Untangling, what a ridiculous method!"

Part Three: The Powers of Presence

They might not even believe what they're saying; it's a strategy, not an expression of a truly held opinion. Think of a police officer standing in front of a crime scene, saying to passers-by, "Move along, folks, nothing to see here," when, of course, there is plenty happening behind the tape.

The Protector doesn't actually believe nothing is there. In fact, it believes the opposite. It believes there is something truly dangerous there, and you are starting to get way too close.

Sticks and stones

Shaming is another strategy Protectors use to try to stop you from going further. They may tell you that you are flawed, defective, broken, sick, crazy. Why on earth would they be so mean to you?

All that nasty name-calling is a strategy. The more frightened your Protectors are, the more vicious their attacks become. The Protector is afraid that what you might find if you go any deeper in yourself will be worse than anything you would feel from it calling you stupid, or lazy, or a failure. It's afraid that if you got in touch with whatever is hidden deep inside, you could be completely destroyed. By its calculation, it's better to feel bad from being called a few names than to be utterly annihilated.

When you are under attack like this, you are (actually a Part of you is) likely to feel small, humiliated, and ashamed. Feeling ashamed is an extremely unpleasant feeling that most people do almost anything to avoid, so this strategy can be highly effective. Instead of going deeper, you might easily become swamped by trying to deal with all the feelings of shame and self-loathing the Protector has stirred up.

A Defender's last-ditch efforts

When you get closer to the core of your Tangle, Defenders will do anything to keep you from experiencing what they fear will be too much for you. Whether it is directly experiencing the feelings of a Small One or the stuck, frozen core of your Tangle, they have developed a host of tactics to stop you in your tracks.

Switcheroo

When a Defender feels you are getting too close to what's at the core of the Tangle, it will do its best to take your awareness in another direction.

Last-Ditch Efforts

A Defender has a whole host of tricks up this particular sleeve.

You already know that a Defender can hijack you. If it thinks you're getting too close to the core, it will just go ahead and do those things that it knows will block or numb your emotions, such as digging into the ice cream or zealously exercising or playing just one more game of solitaire.

Have you ever had a sudden overwhelming feeling that cleaning your closet is the most important thing you can do? Right now? Never mind that you have guests coming or the deadline for your project is looming, you find yourself pulling everything out into heaps on the floor and going through it all. It's amazing how many closets get cleaned when people start getting close to the core of their Tangle!

Swept away on a tide of emotion

Emotion is a way we know what matters to us. It connects us with others and the world. It gives our lives color and vibrancy. However, when you have felt the same emotions about the same thing a hundred times before, getting carried away by those feelings over and over again comes from a Defender directing you away from the core of your Tangle.

When a Defender doesn't want you to get close to something, it may send floods of tears or red-hot anger boiling up to keep you from going there. A person who is sobbing their heart out certainly looks like someone having a genuine emotion. But a Part of them may be intent on making sure they are not feeling something else.

Last-ditch efforts used by both Protectors and Defenders

Protectors and Defenders use some similar strategies to prevent you from getting closer to the core of the Tangle.

Shut down

You don't feel a thing. It's all just kind of empty in there. But it's not a nice, spacious, open, fluid emptiness full of possibility and life. It is an "I don't feel anything" kind of emptiness. It's an "I feel dead inside" kind of emptiness.

Both Protectors and Defenders can deaden your ability to feel your body and your emotions. Either one can be worried about what might happen if you start feeling things. In order to have an empathic relationship with the Part that is shutting you down, you don't have to know if it's a Protector or a Defender. Just say: "Hello, I know you're there, and I sense you don't want me to feel something."

Blockade

Blockading is a strategy both Defenders and Protectors use to create barriers between you and whatever they are worried you are getting close to.

When you first encounter a blockade, it might not be obvious whether it is a Protector or a Defender that is blocking you from going further. Defenders *become*—and Protectors *create*—metaphorical inner walls, eggs, caves, boxes, shells, curtains, blankets, or locked doors, to name just a few possibilities.

Is it a Defender or a Protector creating a barrier? Here's how you can tell:

- Defenders are protecting what is behind the barricade *from* you. They are afraid that you are a harsh or manipulative Protector who will attack or try to change what they are protecting.

- Protectors are protecting *you* from what is behind the barricade. They are afraid that you are a weak Defender who will become overwhelmed by what is there.

They both need your empathy for what they are not wanting to happen if they aren't there taking care of you. Defenders need empathy for what they don't want to have happen if a harsh Protector attacks the tender place they are protecting. And Protectors need empathy for what they don't want to happen to you if you get overwhelmed by the "weak, needy" feelings that are behind the barrier—or, what they are worried would happen if you become merged with that helpless Part.

Checking out

There is an even more extreme form of shutting down which is called dissociation, in which you feel like you have left your body. If you are aware there is a Part of you that sometimes uses dissociation to try to keep you safe, you can become sensitive to early signals that something in you may be about to dissociate. There might be a sense of "This is too much" or "I've got to get out of here."

When a Part starts to send you away from your body, the first step is to pause. Slow right down. Don't keep doing whatever you were doing. Instead acknowledge: "Something in me is finding this too much." You may need to spend a lot of time cultivating Self-in-Presence until you can reliably find places in your body that feel okay, before going further with the Untangling process. You may need to open your eyes and connect with the world around you here and now until you feel more resourced and grounded in Self-in-Presence.

If you do stay with the Untangling process, it's time to set up camp. There is no rush. Make a nice cup of tea (whether literally or otherwise) and sit back to keep company with the Part that is trying to send you out of your body as a way to keep you safe. You're neither moving forward toward whatever is scaring it nor abandoning it. Your message to it is, "I am here with you now."

And you might need to check "in the bushes" for any Parts that are wanting you to go faster. If a Part is resisting, there's likely to be another Part somewhere pushing. They all need to be invited to come and sit at the campfire with you.

Be prepared to make a lot of tea, put your feet up and do a lot of listening! Untangling has its own timetable that you can trust.

"A wall? Okay! Where's the dynamite?"

Whether it's a wall, a locked door or a curtain, often other Parts will want to blow up the wall, find the key for the door or yank back the curtain. By now you know this doesn't help. The blockade will only get stronger. Instead of the wall being merely ten feet tall, now you can't see the top, and it goes on for miles and miles in both directions, or the door now has ten locks and the curtain is nailed to the wall.

Parts that want to push past an obstacle need to be acknowledged and included with *The Power of And*. They also need *The Power of Deep Empathy* so their fears and dreams for you are heard. This will also help the Part that has generated the barricade to calm down.

We love walls!

Walls are so easy to create a relationship with. Whenever you encounter a wall (or other barricade) in your inner world, it's time to put the kettle on again. You might be here for a while. Grab your cup of tea/coffee/matcha and your cushions and imagine yourself leaning up against this inner wall.

Part Three: The Powers of Presence

And now that *you* are comfortable, extend your senses into how the wall is feeling from its point of view. Maybe it feels determined... or worried... or fierce... or something else. When you treat a wall like a sentient, sensitive, living being, it will respond. After all, it is a Part of you. So it's not surprising you can sense how it is feeling.

As a wall comes to trust you—including trusting that you are not going to try to break through it—it will begin to reveal what is behind it. At some point, it is likely to transform utterly, revealing a whole world beyond it.

BARBARA: I was getting close to something painful and delicate. Suddenly I was aware of a wall appearing. It towered over me, stretching out as far as I could see in both directions. Its cold, flat, grey bulk completely blocked me from going any further. So I stopped. "Okay. That's interesting," I thought.

I knew that everything that I experienced inside was likely to be either a manifestation of Self-in-Presence or a form a Part of me is taking. So, in my inner world, I walked up to the wall and gently put my hand up to touch it. It felt warm, like it was alive. I rested my head against it and opened to sensing how it was feeling.

I could sense its determined refusal to let me go further. And I could sense its surprise that I wasn't trying to push past it, that I was being curious and caring with it. I told it I would not push. I knew it had some good reason to be so big and strong right here.

I just waited, telling it how much I appreciated its strength and determination to keep me safe. My heart opened toward this warm, living monolithic being inside me. I kept my awareness there and continued to sense how it was feeling.

Several minutes later I started to feel something beginning to change—and then the wall disappeared. One second it was there, and the next second there was a verdant valley, full of flowers. Sunshine sparkled on a stream flowing through the center of a vast meadow. The air was vibrant with life, my body hummed with delight.

I still don't know what it was afraid would happen if it wasn't there as a wall. It might have been afraid that feeling wonderful would have been too much for me. What it was afraid of doesn't matter now. Everything changed in that moment and I was no longer living in the same world.

I still think lovingly of that wall. I still appreciate how it cared for me diligently for all those years and how graciously it vanished when it no longer needed to protect me.

Don't believe everything you think

Protectors can seem so certain and confident in their point of view. They make flat, definitive statements in a tone that sounds authoritatively final. For example, "This is never going to work!"

It can be easy to get caught up in debating whether something a Part says is true or not. Don't get drawn in to the debate. It will get you nowhere. Why? Because an assertion like "This is never going to work," made by a Protector, is functional. It is strategic. It's meant to have an effect.

Like a lever, it's meant to move something. Debating whether it's true or false will keep you from touching the places where the transformation of a Tangle can happen.

Don't believe everything you feel

Defenders, like Protectors, could be trying to make you believe something for a strategic purpose; while Protectors use words and ideas, Defenders use emotions and body sensations. Defenders can fill your body with undeniably real feelings such as anger or heaviness or sadness. These too can feel like they point to "the truth."

Our student Darius told us about feeling nauseated whenever he thought about his upcoming divorce mediation. He recognized that Part of him was giving him feelings of nausea to keep his awareness away from the whole issue. He spent time listening to that Part of him and discovered what it was afraid the ending of his marriage might mean about who he was as a person. When he did this, the nausea lifted. He was then able to sense more deeply into what was underlying those fears.

What do last-ditch Protectors need from you?

When you are deep in process and suddenly you get sleepy, or you are overcome with inner fog, or you go blank, your relationship needs to be with the Part creating these phenomena. You can say hello to a Part that

Part Three: The Powers of Presence

is using sleepiness to protect you. You can say hello to a Part that creates inner fog or makes you go blank.

When you are being shown scary things, like dead babies or disaster movies of terrible things happening to your loved ones, you can easily get pulled into wondering about what they mean or whether they are real or prophetic. The point is that the Protector is showing you that scary thing to distract or frighten you, to get you to stop.

Don't try to push these Protector Parts away or go past them. They consider themselves your Safety Guardians and, in a very real way, they are. They are motivated entirely by concern for your safety—and until now, they were your best chance for staying inwardly safe.

Once you are in a relationship with a last-ditch Protector, you can respectfully and compassionately invite this Protector to let you know what it fears will happen if you go further. It will probably tell you something like, "I don't want you to suffer forever and ever. I don't want you to be destroyed. I don't want you to go crazy and be locked up for the rest of your life."

That is the kind of thing it thinks it is protecting you from. It needs your deep empathy. Keep sensing what it's not wanting until it relaxes and you can go further.

Even if it steps aside or waves you on, it might also say, "But I will be watching." That's fine. You can even invite the Protector to sit beside you as you turn toward the Part of you that it has been shielding you from.

What do last-ditch Defenders need from you?

When Defenders are scared, they are scared right now. For them, whatever is happening is happening in this moment. For them, past and present are one and the same. The most important thing you can do to help them is to cultivate Self-in-Presence.

When you can keep company with a scared Defender without merging with it, the Defender becomes more and more confident in your ability to go deeper and remain present as yourself. Eventually it will trust that you can feel whatever needs to be felt and you will still be okay.

To help a Defender gain confidence in your ability to experience whatever needs your awareness, sense how it needs you to be with it and then follow its lead. As you keep sensing how it is responding to you, you will be able to sense it starting to trust you.

Developing a relationship like this with a Defender is healing in its own right. This kind of sensitive, empathic relationship was missing when you became entangled in the first place.

As your Defenders come to trust your gentleness and strength, you will find yourself naturally living in freer, less Tangled ways.

Despair

There's one more kind of thing that can happen as you get close to the frozen core of your Tangle. You may get in touch with a kind of overwhelming despair when a Part of you truly believes that change is impossible. It grieves for all the life that has passed you by, unfulfilled. Lost forever. It feels that nothing will ever be better. It says things like, "It's never changed yet. Why would it change now? You've tried so hard for years and years, and it's just hopeless. It's awful and it will always be like this."

Despair is often experienced as an intensely unpleasant body feeling. When you have that sinking feeling like lead weights dragging you down or like there's a thick, wet blanket covering you so you can barely breathe, that seems to be how you are feeling.

The more strongly you feel something in your body, the more likely you are to merge with it. Unmerging from a Part in this kind of deep despair can be extremely challenging. At the same time, getting in touch with it can be deeply painful. You'll need all your Powers of Presence not to merge with it and believe it.

If you are merged with it, you may feel as if you've finally found out the horrible truth about your Tangle: you will never be free of it. But instead of feeling relief, which is what you experience when you empathically understand the deepest truth of what a Part of you most dreads, you feel terrible.

This despairing Part feels utterly alone, and it can't imagine how this could ever change. It may be right on the edge of believing that the only thing you can do is to give up altogether. In its eyes, the future looks totally bleak.

Unmerging from a Part in despair is doubly difficult because it seems to be about what is self-evidently real and true. Its despair is all tangled up with what it is afraid is the rock-bottom truth about you and the world.

When a Part makes categorical statements about how something is or how you are, listen for the emotion behind the words. You do not need to defend yourself against its accusations. You do not need to counter its bleak view of the world by pointing out all the good things in your life.

You can be in responsive and empathic contact with a despairing Part without being taken over by it. When it says, "It's never going to change!" you can respond with something like, "I really hear how afraid you are that it's never going to change."

This Part needs your company and your empathy for just how difficult life is for it. When you empathically listen to the fears behind its words, it experiences the kind of relationship it has always been searching for. Eventually it will feel the relief that comes from knowing you have heard the depths of its fears without running away or trying to change it. In that moment, it is able to heal and transform.

Give them a medal—and Deep Empathy

Distracting your attention, sending you brain fog, heading to the refrigerator, putting up inner barriers and walls, and more... aren't these what's often called "resistance"? Indeed they are.

There's a popular idea that resistance is something you should overcome. You may have thought you needed to push through or push past resistance in order to get unstuck.

We don't think so. Instead, we would say, *"Vive la résistance!"*

All these strategies are desperate attempts to keep you safe, made by well-meaning and terrified Parts of you. Trying to strong-arm past them doesn't work because, from their point of view, they are not saboteurs but heroes.

You need all your Powers when you are faced with these Parts but perhaps the most important one is *The Power of Deep Empathy*. For your Parts to be able to change, they need to feel confident that you can understand their deepest fears without shaming, manipulating, undermining, punishing, or pushing them. They need to know that things are different now.

You're not that younger person who couldn't handle the unnameable, unimaginably scary stuff that your Parts believe is "down there." As you develop your Powers of Presence, you strengthen the resources you need to go to the heart of your Tangle.

As you spend time empathizing with Protectors and Defenders, you may be able to sense something else hovering at the edge of your awareness. It may be blurry or out of focus, just out of reach. Striving to bring it into focus won't work. It will become clearer naturally when you are able to keep company with the Part that is using its last-ditch efforts to keep you away from something. When that Part eventually trusts you to be able to go there without being destroyed, it will finally let you connect with what it has been protecting you from.

It turns out that the deeper level—what a Part thought would destroy you—holds a powerful gift for your transformation and your freedom.

Part Three: The Powers of Presence

Chapter 17
THE THAWING OF THE FROZEN CORE

BARBARA: I had spent a lot of time with the Part of me that climbed into bed whenever I was under stress—and that had helped. By now I was able to do my job as a freelance graphic designer, take care of my daughter and myself, and teach Focusing. But sometimes something would knock me off-balance, and I'd be back under the covers again.

Ann and I had had success Untangling other issues, so I decided to spend some time with the Part of me that retreated to my bed. I could sense something in me felt it was completely impossible to be myself in the world. As I brought my awareness to it, I could feel an intense pressure and a kind of pain in my solar plexus. I moved my hands to gently rest there.

I was able to stay with this Part, to let it know that I could sense how everything felt too hard and too painful for it. I could sense how much it appreciated my being there with it, understanding how painful this had been for it. It started to relax.

Then I began to sense something else. At first I thought it might be another Part, but it wasn't Part-like. There was no emotion. It had no belief about me or the world. It was more like an impenetrable inner barrier. Movement through it or around it was impossible.

Coming up to this barrier was like coming to the end of the world.

Only one thing was possible. I could stay with it and sense it, exactly as it was, and find just the right words or images that would fit it perfectly.

Life is process. Living means always getting ready for what needs to happen next. When you inhale, you are getting ready to exhale. When you eat, your body is getting ready to digest. As long as you are alive, there is always something that comes next, whether it's a nap or a smile from a loved one or a chance to learn something.

Part Three: The Powers of Presence

But what we need so our next step of life is possible doesn't always happen. Say something difficult happens... and your life stops moving forward in the way that would be right. Your body has a feeling of that forward momentum of life being stopped.

We've all gone through lots of experiences that were tough in one way or another. They may have even been as hard as having a serious accident, getting fired or laid off unexpectedly, having your house burn down, being really sick, losing someone you love. They may have been less dramatic, seemingly less important, like being told there's no room for you in the car by the people you thought were your best friends, or knowing people are talking about you behind your back, or not being able to take your troubles and worries to anyone without being dismissed or ridiculed. In any case, what would have been really right for your life's next steps becomes impossible.

Naturally you will also have an emotional reaction to being stopped. You might feel frustrated or bewildered or upset or sad or angry or scared about it. These emotional reactions are a natural part of your body's response to not being able to take the next steps of your life in the way that would be right for you.

Your body-mind can process the experience of being stopped—what that feels like in your body and the emotions about it—if you have the resources to do that, or if you get the right kind of support from someone else. If that happens you will be able to live beyond where your life has been interrupted.

But if it is impossible for you to bear the emotions that arise in response to being stopped, your emotional reaction to not being able to live forward becomes frozen in time. When feelings are frozen, they cannot be felt, nor can they shift and evolve. What should have been a straightforward, if painful, experience has now become impossible to live beyond.

It's a Stoppage—and around it, a Tangle forms.

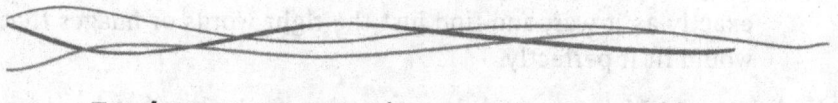

Tangles are a stoppage in process—not a problem in understanding.

A Stoppage isn't a Part

A Part has a point of view. It has its own emotions. A Part wants or doesn't want something, often passionately and urgently. Parts struggle with other Parts, or collaborate with them. Parts hide, or they assert their presence loudly.

A Stoppage isn't like that. It doesn't have emotions or a point of view. It's not "someone" inside you. If you get quiet and pay attention and spend time with your Parts until they calm down, you can begin to feel a Stoppage. But it's more like a "something" than a "someone." And it will never talk to you. It doesn't need a relationship with you. It needs something else.

The Power of Felt-Sensing the Stoppage

You could look at a Stoppage as how something is stuck in your life. In that view, a Stoppage might seem like a set of external circumstances that need to be fixed, changed, controlled. But what if you see a Stoppage not as a problem to be solved but as your body's way of carrying the potential for life to move forward fully in the way it should have done back then?

What is needed so that a Stoppage can transform is our fourth Power: *The Power of Felt-Sensing the Stoppage.* It's based on an ability you may not have heard much about before: *felt-sensing.*

Developed by Eugene Gendlin from his research into successful change processes in psychotherapy, and from his background in philosophy, including phenomenology, felt-sensing is a way to directly experience how your body "has" the whole of something—whether it is a creative project or a decision or the Stoppage at the heart of a Tangle.

Felt-sensing is a transformational process in itself. When a felt sense forms, a real resolution for what had seemed impossibly stuck only moments before can happen.

When a felt sense shifts, something that cannot be predicted from within the Tangle can spontaneously emerge. It is a carrying-forward of the Tangled situation that is new, fresh and satisfyingly fits your current situation.

What is a felt sense?

An artist stands in front of a painting she is working on. She is stuck. She doesn't know what the right next step is.

She sets down her brush and stands back, taking it all in. She pauses to let a sense of the painting come. This sense of the painting needs a little time to form. A felt sense is not the feeling you already have about something. It is a fresh sense that comes now, when you pause and invite it.

Her felt sense includes everything about this painting: what she sees in front of her, her vision and intention for the painting, as well as what the problem is and what the painting needs next. All of this is felt in her body as one whole, multifaceted experience. When a felt sense comes, it isn't easy to put into words. She may need to sit patiently with her felt sense of the painting until the next step reveals itself.

When her felt sense of the painting shifts, the artist now knows what the next step is. She doesn't have to figure it out. "I just knew," she says later. She could say things about what the problem was and what she can now do, but she doesn't have to say anything. She is now able to pick up her brush and get back to the canvas.

In this example, the felt sense was about a creative project, making a work of art. But you can pause and get a felt sense of anything: a decision, a relationship, a whole situation that you're in—or a Stoppage.

Felt-Sensing a Stoppage

What does the felt sense of a Stoppage feel like? It is often surprisingly delicate, vague, not very strong, especially at first. It is usually felt somewhere in the middle of your body, in the area from your throat to your groin. It might feel strange, vague, mysterious, like it's not going anywhere. Usually, there are no words that capture it easily. You just feel *something*.

Though the feeling of what the Stoppage is like is often not clear at all, if you stay with it, something clearly is there. It takes patience to be with something that seems so elusive and yet so unchanging. You'll need all your Self-in-Presence to stay with it without merging with Parts that are attempting to escape it or figure it out or change it.

Felt-sensing a Stoppage has only a few steps. Everything you've done in Untangling up until now has prepared you for this: being able to sense the Stoppage in your body exactly as it is, and symbolize it precisely.

The Thawing of the Frozen Core

Sensing in your body

Take time to sense the Stoppage in your body exactly as it is. This is the direct experience of how a needed next step of living was impossible—and still is. Sense every nuance of this impossible step you are capable of experiencing in your body. Notice precisely where the sensations are, notice their texture, their color, if they have an emotional quality.

Whatever words come to describe this experience, say "yes" to them. They don't have to be accurate or factual or make sense. Treat them as metaphorical pointers to a deeper, more precise development of the felt sense. Accepting whatever comes allows a next step to happen.

To demonstrate these steps, we'll share a transcript of an Untangling session Barbara had when she was felt-sensing a Stoppage.

BARBARA: This place in my body feels shaky... kind of sick... kind of like a strung-out addict going cold turkey. There is an image of a person lying on a bed, being sick, sweating and shivering.

If you can, stay there as long as something still needs attention. Take your time to acknowledge that this is what has been impossible to feel. Acknowledge you are feeling it now.

BARBARA: There is a feeling of lost... a lost feeling stretching back in time... so far...so far.... All that time lost. And now we're left with this—this sick, shivering person lying on a bed.

I'm acknowledging that this is here now, this is how it feels. It is quite uncomfortable—and I am okay. Somehow this is what I couldn't feel before.

At first, Barbara wasn't sure whether this was a Part or a Stoppage. As she stayed with it, she could tell that this was what imagining living beyond an inner barrier felt like in her body, so it was less like a Part, and more like a felt sense of a Stoppage.

Finding a symbol

The next step is to symbolize what you are experiencing as precisely and accurately as possible. When you start to directly sense in your body what "impossible" feels like, you can start to sense for metaphors and symbols that match it exactly.

Part Three: The Powers of Presence

BARBARA: I am staying with it, sensing what this feeling in my body is *like*... and the words come: It almost feels like something got destroyed. Like somebody reached into me and took something and broke it. Like somebody reached inside my body and took this... this compass, this way-finding device, this pathfinding ability... and they took it out and broke it.

That brought a deep breath when she said those words.

It feels awful... and it's a relief to get the words that fit.

It's important to remember that the symbol doesn't need to make any sense. It just needs to match the felt sense of the Stoppage. There's a big temptation to try to hurry this process along by making up symbols, or guessing at them, or trying to figure out what they mean. Be patient! Trying to go faster will slow you down.

Instead, take all the time you need to sense for the symbol that captures this felt-in-your-body experience exactly. The symbol can take any form. It might be a single word or short phrase, but it is likely to be a surprising metaphor, an image, a sound, a gesture, or body posture.

BARBARA: There is a feeling of a bottomless pit opening out beneath me. The image of a bomb going off, destroying me. Being blown to bits. It's like standing in the center of a blast zone. A kind of white noise. Everything stops.

And I'm just staying with it.

Remember, this experience has never been able to be fully felt before. Both the actual experience of the Stoppage and the symbols that fit it precisely and exactly need time to form.

Sometimes you have to keep tapping into this place for hours or even days before you find the symbolization that fits it completely.

You will know when this happens—the shift is unmistakable. After some minutes of continuing to stay with the feeling of being blown to bits as fully and exactly as possible, this happened:

BARBARA: Oh! Wow! It's a kind of body bliss and breathtaking energy like a sun blazing from my solar plexus... shimmering through my whole body... and out to the edges of the universe... and that only hints at what it is like.

The Thawing of the Frozen Core

The Power of Felt-Sensing the Stoppage

1. You can feel there is something in you that doesn't have emotions or a point of view and feels utterly immovable.

2. Cultivate your ability to be Self-in-Presence by sensing how your body is being supported. Sense what feels good (at ease, flowing, relaxed) in your body right now.

3. With your awareness in your throat, chest, stomach area, let the sense of what is impossibly immovable be there, unformed, unclear, without words at first. Settle down to spend time with the felt sense of the Stoppage, no hurry, no need for anything to change.

4. When you're ready, begin to describe what it is like. Use words, images, gestures, or metaphors to capture its essential quality. Images that come can often be seen as metaphorical representations of what the time of the Stoppage felt like.

5. Check if the description is a good match for the felt sense. Let the description change until it fits. This takes time.

6. There may or may not be a shift in how the felt sense feels. If there isn't by the time it is time to stop, thank your body and your body's process—and plan to return and spend more time.

7. If there if a positive shift in how the felt sense feels, take time to receive it.

Living forward

Paradoxically—and rather wonderfully—the closer you get to the place where something in your life feels absolutely impossible, the closer you are to your Tangle untangling itself.

Coming up against what feels "impossible" means you're exactly where

Part Three: The Powers of Presence

you need to be in order for your Tangle to evolve into freedom and choice rather than be mired in limitation and burden.

We've seen this happen so often that we now get delighted when we encounter the feeling of something being "impossible." When it feels like you have come to the end of the road, you are actually at the place where change happens.

When the Stoppage is felt and symbolized exactly as it is, it shifts. Often there is an astonishing and seemingly miraculous transformation that occurs when a symbol matches the felt sense precisely. Just as happened for Barbara, you can shift from darkest pain to radiant aliveness in the space of a heartbeat. This is a lived, whole-body experience of transformation.

What becomes possible was unimaginable only moments before. This is so much more than just feeling better. Because your body is part of a complex interactional situation, when your body changes, what is possible in that situation and many other situations in your life changes as well.

You won't be able to figure out logically what you can do now. That's too complex even for supercomputers to handle. Your whole body will now be free to respond spontaneously in ways that will fit the situation in the best way possible.

Our student Felicity found herself having a calm conversation with her sister for the first time in forty years. And Laurence found himself speaking in public without even remembering it used to be hard for him. Ann found herself having comfortable friendships with men without any aura of longing or unfulfilled desire. Barbara now sees beauty all around her in the flight of a bird, or in someone's smile, or the way light moves through the leaves, and she is filled with a profound sense of being vibrantly alive—a feeling that is precious beyond measure.

If you're patient and persistent, your Untangling Powers will bring you to the experience of the Stoppage. Since the Stoppage is here now, it can change now. Just as it's never too late for your relationship with your Parts to heal, it's never too late for a Stoppage to transform. There is no way to force this to happen. It happens on its own. When the Stoppage shifts, the Tangle untangles itself.

Chapter 18
WIDENING THE HORIZON

We'd been working on this book for over three years, and it was getting close to being finished. Each chapter had been separately gone over and polished. There were only a few chapters left to complete. But when we tried working on those remaining chapters, we got stuck. They didn't work. Progress ground to a halt.

Going chapter by chapter had led to a complete impasse. We had to pause and get a felt sense of the whole book. Only then did the problem become clear. The result: a major restructuring that (we think) made the book much better. What was needed only emerged from sensing the book as a whole.

Tangles are like that, too. When you have been working with a Tangle for a while, you might get so immersed in being with particular Parts that you can feel like you're wandering around in circles. Protectors say this, Defenders do that, Small Ones peek out and withdraw into hiding again... You go deep with different Parts, and even if there is some relief, you don't know what's truly changed.

When you are working with a Tangle, every so often it helps to shift your level of awareness. So it is time to introduce you to our last Power of Untangling: *The Power of Felt-Sensing it All*. In this fifth Power you will be getting a felt sense of the whole Tangle.

When you are *Felt-Sensing It All,* you will be acknowledging every aspect of your Tangle that you are currently aware of. You will be inviting everything in your life that is included in your Tangle, even if you don't see how it is relevant.

When you pause with the intention of sensing-the-whole-and-more, a felt sense of your Tangle can form.

By getting a felt sense of the whole, you are shifting out of the narrow world of your Tangle into a wider field of awareness where new possibilities can emerge.

Part Three: The Powers of Presence

The whole is greater than the sum of its Parts

Although we have been talking about Parts and how to relate to them in ways that help them heal, you are, in essence, a whole, undivided living being. Your Tangle lives in your body as a complete living process.

The situations you are engaged in are also living processes. Every aspect of your life is influenced by your situations. And you affect every situation as well. And, because situations are intricately interrelated living processes, you can't simply remove one factor in a situation and replace it with another.

In *The Power of Felt-Sensing It All,* you consciously and deliberately invite everything that is somehow relevant in your Tangle to come together in one felt experience: memories of similar situations, thoughts about it all, Parts you've become aware of, other people's reactions, and even more. And then, rather than dealing with each aspect separately, you pause so a felt sense of the Tangled situation as a whole can form.

The process of *Felt-Sensing It All* will take you to a completely different level, one where you are not mired in the patterns and assumptions of the Tangle. Your body actually changes, and this physical shift in how your body carries your Tangle allows you to live in ways that had not been available before, taking actions that are right for you and that move the whole situation forward.

The Pink Silk Arrow-Cushion

ANN: When I sat down in front of the group to demonstrate the new exercise Barbara had created, I had no suspicion at all that my whole life, even my appearance, was about to transform.

My Tangle was about how impossible it was for me to feel comfortable wearing professional clothes.

I longed to be a public speaker, and give messages of hope and inspiration to large audiences. But books on public speaking emphasized the importance of looking professional. That meant wearing "nice" clothes—and my relationship with clothes was a troubled one. I hated clothes shopping. I felt judged just walking into a clothing store, as if the clothes themselves were criticizing me. "Nice" clothes felt stiff and uncomfortable; I could only feel like myself in casual clothes. The thought of standing up in front of a crowd in my drab, ill-fitting, casual clothes was uncomfortable, but I was even more uncomfortable thinking about wearing anything else.

It was a Tangle—and because of it, my dream of becoming a public speaker felt impossible. But more than that: in *every* public situation—teaching a workshop, chairing a meeting, networking at a conference—there was always a part of me that was not sure I belonged. Not sure I was okay. Not sure I was worthy, even after all my accomplishments. The clothes I wore—or couldn't wear—were somehow a symbol of all that.

Like all Tangles, it was both about the obvious issue, my clothes, and also about something much bigger and deeper. My very identity and sense of self-worth were at stake.

I had already given a lot of Deep Empathy to several Parts in this Tangle by the time we sat down that day. I'd connected with early experiences of being bullied and mocked at school for somehow wearing the wrong clothes. I'd given gentle, loving company to the younger me who went through those painful experiences.

Barbara started by inviting me to gather—both remembering and sensing—all the elements and aspects of the Tangle about clothes and being myself in the world.

I felt judged and uncomfortable in clothing stores, feeling stiff and not myself in "nice" clothes, the younger me who was ridiculed for what she wore, the time in fifth grade when my teacher told me I ought to wear dresses to school or people would talk, my longing to be a public speaker—including the times when speaking to a group felt wonderful and times when it was scary and disappointing... all of that and more. I said to myself: "This Tangle includes everything I already know about it, and everything I don't know yet."

Having invited all that, I took my time to freshly sense how my body carried this Tangle. Slowly, I began to feel something in the middle area of my body. The instruction in the exercise was "Let it be there without words at first," and that was helpful, because there were certainly no words... except perhaps the word "something." I did feel *something*.

I let it take the time it needed. Slowly I began to feel it more and more distinctly in the middle of my torso. It was forming into something that I could start to describe. The following metaphorical phrases emerged slowly over about ten minutes:

"It's like... a cushion..."

"It's like... an arrow... pointing forward..."

"There's the color pink, and the feeling of silk..."

"It's like a cushion in the shape of an arrow..."

"It's a pink silk arrow-shaped cushion pointing forward!"

Ah! What a strange image! But getting the exact right words for this vividly present image brought an enormous sense of relief and elation. I loved my pink silk arrow-cushion! It was gorgeous! Where had it come from? Who could have invented it? It was certainly not from logical thinking! From all that was included in the whole issue about clothes and being myself in the world, from all the processes that had gone on up until this moment, and my inner sense of what could happen next, *this* is what my body had created.

It was a beautiful moment. The felt sense of the whole Tangle had formed. When the right words emerged that fit perfectly, everything changed.

The next steps emerge

At the end of a *Felt-Sensing It All* process, it is important not to try to make logical sense of the symbols that come that match the felt sense. After all, how logical is a pink silk arrow! But there is something you can do next.

If you feel that something has shifted, it is unlikely you will know exactly what is now different or why it changed. What is now possible will become evident as you live your life. Surprising new possibilities may spontaneously occur to you. You may find yourself feeling completely differently about your life even if your outer circumstances stay the same.

Even so, there is a further invitation you can make, as part of *Felt-Sensing It All*. Our favorite way to phrase this is to ask, "What's possible now that wasn't possible before?" And then allow the answer to come from the felt sense itself.

"I could go into a clothing store—and be curious."

ANN: Then Barbara asked if I would be ready for another invitation. "Sure," I said.

"You might sense," she said, "what feels possible now that wasn't possible before."

Even before I tried doing what she suggested, I could feel it was the perfect invitation. I paused... making sure that I was sensing my body's response instead of answering "from the head." After a few minutes, some words spontaneously came: "I could go into a clothing store—*and be curious.*"

I took some time to enjoy the sense of rightness that came with those words and thanked my body. And that was the end of the session.

The rest of that day, and the next day, and the next, nothing was outwardly different. I had enjoyed the process and I let it go. I didn't know what would happen in my life, and I didn't worry about it.

It was when I got home again that things began to change. Without really thinking much about it, I asked a close friend if she would go shopping with me. The first store we went into, I could tell just by walking once through the racks of clothes that these styles were not for me, so we left.

I had no feeling of being judged by the clothes, merely feeling these were not for me. In the next store, I was drawn to some colors and styles. There was one suit in a light green that reminded me of springtime, in a beautifully soft fabric I kept wanting to touch. I tried it on... felt good wearing it... and bought it.

The next weekend, I got a feeling about a shopping area in a different town, a sense I might find something there. Again I asked my friend to go with me, and we visited a few different boutiques before we found one that clicked. The styles, colors, and fabrics spoke to me. There was also a helpful store employee, who kept finding me perfect things to try on. I walked out that day with ten items, feeling elated. All of them were flowing, comfortable, stylish, and suitable to wear on stage.

Then I found myself asking, what hairstyle was I drawn to? I noticed what styles I liked while watching TV. I clipped pictures

Part Three: The Powers of Presence

from magazines. I took them with me on my next visit to my hair stylist—and she pulled it all together into a cut that was both relaxed and professional.

Something interesting to notice is how often I asked for and received help, both from people I knew and people I didn't know. When I'd been mired in my Tangle, I wouldn't have done that. Tangles are isolating. Life is connecting.

About three months into this process, I went to a Focusing conference. I wore my stylish new clothes, shoes and jewelry, feeling comfortable and confident in how I looked. Most of all, I had the inner sense of fun, enjoyment and elation at being myself while meeting the world. The reactions I got from people who had known me for years were remarkable. Heads were turning, mouths were dropping open. Had I lost weight? Was I in love? I just smiled.

Around that same time, I got an invitation to be a keynote speaker at a conference for psychotherapists in New York. My first keynote! I shared the stage with people I admired, felt confident and calm, and my talk was well received. So much had opened up and become possible! And, I would emphasize, these have been lasting changes. That Tangle has untangled... for good.

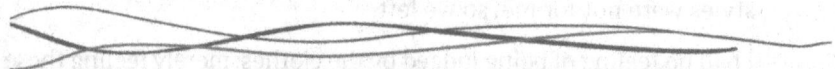

The Power of Felt-Sensing It All

1. Take time to invite everything included in your Tangle: emotions, situations where you get stuck, Parts, memories, difficulties, what you want to be different. Let it all gather in your awareness without going into any specific aspect of it.

2. Say to yourself, "I'm sensing everything I already know about this Tangle and everything I don't yet know."

3. With your awareness in your throat, chest, stomach, and abdomen, invite the felt sense of the whole Tangle to form freshly. Give it time. Be patient. After a while, you'll be aware that something is there. Let it be there, unformed, unclear, without words.

4. When you're ready, begin to describe what it is like. Use words, images, gestures, or metaphors to capture its essential quality.

5. Check if the description of the felt sense is a good match. Let the description change until it fits. This also takes time.

6. After you get a satisfying sense of "Yes, it fits," notice what's possible now that wasn't possible before.

Living beyond the Tangle

When the felt sense of a whole Tangle forms, you are *already* living beyond what has felt eternally stuck. You "have" your previously Tangled situation in a new way. How you think about it, what you feel and what you are able to do will all be different now. Often the knowing of what needs to happen next simply comes to you. You find that you are acting freely in those situations in which you had felt utterly bound.

When a Tangle changes, it changes as an organism changes, not as a machine does. When it shifts, it all changes together. There is both greater complexity *and* simplicity. Where before there was a confusion of many disparate and disconnected Parts, now a natural sense of wholeness forms. Where there was narrow rigidity, there is now creative flexibility.

Part Four
Living Free

Now, you are the new living that is ongoing.
Eugene Gendlin, *Focusing-Oriented Psychotherapy*, p. 21

When a Tangle untangles, every aspect of your life is affected. The whole mesh of your life is different. Changes ripple out in ways you had never imagined as you embody this new way of being. Your situations are no longer the same situations, because you are no longer the same person. How you hold yourself, how you behave, how you respond to what happens to you—all these and more have all changed. In essence, you are living in the world in a new body.

This type of change is not something you can bring about by planning and willpower. You live it forward. The shift in your body carries you forward into a changed life. You are more able to live with serenity, patience, humor, and courage in situations that were impossibly difficult before.

This is what it is like to live more and more as your whole, free, natural self.

Part Four: Living Free

Chapter 19
LIFE EMERGING

BARBARA: Leaning against the mossy old gate, gazing out into the woodsmoke-scented autumn woods, I saw all the beauty of the majestic golden and russet oak forest around me. I felt the soft cool breeze on my cheek as it rustled through the leaves still clinging to the branches. I breathed in the spice of leaves and smoke. But I felt dead inside. None of the loveliness that surrounded me touched those sad and anxious places inside me. The only thing I felt was frustration. I couldn't take in any of the abundant beauty around me no matter how hard I tried.

This was many, many years ago.

This morning, I got out of bed and pushed up the blind. In the east the dawn was painting the sky with peach, raspberry, hints of ruby and sapphire, glimmering through the dark lace of winter branches. I drank in its radiant beauty, feeling it wash through me. As I turned from the window, my body was filled with glowing aliveness, carrying me into my day.

When something significant shifts in a Tangle, sometimes you know it right away. Sometimes there are dramatic changes that are so obvious that you and everyone in your life notices. But sometimes it is more as if the texture of your life has changed in subtle ways that are hard to describe. Little by little these changes accumulate until, as you look back, you can see what a difference there is now. Over time, barely noticeable shifts can profoundly change the whole nature of what it is to be you in the world.

Whether the shifts in your Tangle are dramatic or subtle, Untangling means that your feelings, thoughts, and perceptions change. So do your relationships—because when one person changes at this deep fundamental level, that changes how everyone in the situation relates. As for the situations themselves—well, because you are living in a different way, they can't help but be influenced in some way too, subtly or dramatically.

Part Four: Living Free

Transformational change

When you were still inside your Tangle, you may have made many changes that didn't actually make any difference to you or your life. Change alone is not what's important. If the ocean liner is sinking, it doesn't help to rearrange the deck chairs! What you need is change that fundamentally transforms you, enabling you to move forward in the direction your life needs to go.

Transformational change occurs in two ways: incremental change which happens gradually and quantum change which happens in sudden and discontinuous leaps.

Little by little

BARBARA: When I was growing up in Manitoba, an unmistakable moment occurred every year sometime in April. The snow still lay mounded in great heaps, grey and dirty, with months of grime ground into it, but one morning there would be a difference. I could smell it.

A hint of spring wafted on the breeze. I knew the thaw had begun, and my body leaned into the promise of summer sun to come.

It still took many days for the snow to crumble and wash away and for crocuses and daffodils to push their green shoots out of the cold earth. There would still be mornings when snowmelt froze into dark sheets of ice, slippery and treacherous underfoot.

The next day a thick layer of shining snow would blanket the world again. And yet, every year, what was implied in that whiff of springtime would eventually come to pass, and the hot, dry days of July would unfold at last.

Like springtime in Manitoba, change can happen one almost imperceptible step at a time, building incrementally into life-changing differences. The shifts can be so tiny they are easy to overlook. It's not until many such shifts have happened that you start to notice there's been a perceptible change.

Even then, Parts might find it hard to believe anything has actually changed. You are most able to recognize those incremental steps of change when you are not identified with a Part.

Whenever you are Self-in-Presence, keeping company with a Part, or getting a felt sense of something, transformational change is already happening—whether or not you can feel it or see it yet.

It changes in an instant

Shifts in your Tangle can be stunning, dramatic and life-shaking. Because everything in your inner world is ongoing, living process, everything in your inner world has the ability to transform. How something *seems to be* is only a form that it is taking right now seen from a particular point of view.

In your inner world, when you are in an Untangling session, things can change with a fluidity and speed that can seem magical. A dagger comes alive and becomes a black panther becomes a ferocious child becomes a strong, mature woman—all in the space of a few moments. A wall becomes an egg becomes a phoenix rising into the sky. A frozen, dead, solid mass of nothing becomes a wave of glorious energy radiating out from your center into the farthest reaches of the universe.

Nonlinear change can seem totally mysterious. Without even thinking about it, you find yourself doing something you had been utterly unable to do before. It is now possible to feel or believe something that had previously been completely impossible.

Our student Lois had a Tangle which included being absolutely unable to meditate. She had been an avid meditator and was even a member of a small Buddhist group, but her own meditating just didn't happen. After months of bringing the Untangling Powers to her Tangle, Lois experienced a transformation that absolutely astonished her.

In her own words: "Some part of me believed that the way I would get back to meditating was through a kind of resolute muscling through: setting a structure, and getting tough on myself to follow it through. But what happened was, without my even realizing this was happening, I spontaneously said to my group, 'Why don't I set up a Zoom group at 7:00 every morning and whoever wants to come, can come.'

"And now I'm meditating five days a week, and I didn't even realize that was going to be the result until I did it. The most amazing thing is that I'm doing it easily, like it's the most natural thing in the world."

You can't force this kind of change. You don't know when or how it will happen. What you do know is how to make the change more likely. Being Self-in-Presence... being patiently present with something you are aware

Part Four: Living Free

of... being with each of your Parts in the way they need... all this creates the environment in which transformational change most easily and naturally occurs.

Five processes of transformation

Ann's story in the last chapter in which her whole appearance changed might make it seem like *Felt-Sensing It All* is the point where an Untangling process has its ultimate transformation. And indeed, *Felt-Sensing It All* can be extraordinarily transformative. But there is not just one place in the Untangling process where transformation happens. There are at least five.

One — Transformation through Not-wanting

When you are empathizing with a Protector or a Defender in the Deep Empathy process (described in Chapter Thirteen, *The Magic of Empathy*), and it feels that its most profound fear is completely heard and understood, there can be an enormous feeling of relief. Often discovering what was most feared is experienced as anticlimactic: "Oh! That's all? That's no big deal! I can live with that." It can bring a huge release of energy and possibility, and what was feared no longer triggers anxiety or aversion.

Two — Transformation through Wanting

During the Deep Empathy process, when you are able to sense what is most deeply Wanted, there can come a moment when you start to experience directly in your body the feeling of aliveness that a Part wants you to be able to feel. At this point it becomes clear that how you feel is not entirely dependent on outer-world circumstances. It's a feeling that's been wanted for a long time, and right now, in this present moment, you are feeling it— uncoupled from what you thought you had to do or to have or be in order to feel it. Something that has been waiting to happen, perhaps even for decades, is happening right now. This is a transformational moment.

Three — Transformation of the Small One

Offering deep empathic company and contact to a Small One (described in Chapter Fifteen, *The Healing Power of Love*) is clearly a transformational process. Ever since the time when the Small One formed, the next step

Life Emerging

of living that needed to happen has not been possible. When you give a Small One the empathic company it needs, that fills in what was missing, emotionally and relationally. The result: the Small One transforms from a Part of you feeling vulnerable and wounded to a vibrant source of exuberant life at the core of your being.

Four — Transformation of the Stoppage

Felt-Sensing the Stoppage (described in Chapter Seventeen, *The Thawing of the Frozen Core*) also allows something to happen that has never happened before. Direct awareness, sensing without judging, taking the time to be present to what is, exactly as it is... all this allows the process that became stuck in the Stoppage to resume its flow. In other words, it is no longer a Stoppage. This is a process that draws on the organismic healing capacity of living beings. The life process, when not interfered with, knows its own way forward.

Five — Transformation through felt-sensing the whole Tangle

Felt-Sensing It All (described in Chapter Eighteen, *Widening the Horizon*) is a way of shifting levels and taking you out beyond the borders of the Tangle into a fresh sense of the whole Tangle that includes everything connected with it, including its larger context. A radical transformation of the whole Tangle becomes possible when you get bigger than the limited strategies and beliefs your Parts have been mired in for so long. You find yourself living in remarkably different ways as new possibilities of thinking, feeling, and acting spontaneously open up for you.

Where green shoots grow

The hint of life changing, moving, shifting, and growing can be almost invisible, not easy to trust or believe in, like that subtle scent of something different in the April air. Here are five places in your Tangle where you can find spring beginning to blossom:

Self-in-Presence

First and foremost, we want to draw your attention to the changes that occur in your ability to embody Self-in-Presence itself. You'll be able to be curious and compassionate toward Parts of you that you used to dislike

Part Four: Living Free

or fear. You'll know you can experience strong feelings without fearing you'll be overwhelmed. You'll become calmer in situations that used to upset or frighten you.

The changes you have been experiencing since you began practicing how to cultivate Self-in-Presence will probably have been gradual, incremental, and not always consistent—rather like springtime in Manitoba. This kind of change requires deliberate practice. Recognizing, Resourcing, and Relating: the more you practice these three pillars of Presence, the stronger your capacity to embody Presence gets. The stronger you become.

Protectors

As you are able to offer your Protectors the kind of understanding they have needed, they will be able to trust you more and more. They begin to see you as separate and different from the Defenders and the Small One in your Tangle. They start to have confidence that you are not going to be taken over by other Parts, at least not for long. The more your Protectors trust you, the less anxious they are.

As you empathize with how hard a Protector Part has worked for you, how lonely it has been, how vilified by other Parts, it softens, and your heart melts. Its ability to notice areas of your life that need attention become your ability to turn toward and deal with what is difficult or challenging.

A Protector can change dramatically and quickly from being an anxiety-ridden, controlling, harsh and critical enemy to being a gentle, loving, supportive and caring ally. Step by step, as you hear what its deepest concerns are, it relaxes more and more. Eventually, it is no longer a separate Part, releasing all its attributes and abilities back into your whole being.

Defenders

And how about Defenders? How do they change?

Remember that Defenders are able to do things. You taking action and a Defender taking action might not be discernibly different from the outside. You might even do exactly the same thing in both cases. But from the inside it can be the difference between night and day.

When you're identified with a Defender, your actions will not arise from your calm, flowing Self responding to what's needed in this present situation.

Life Emerging

What drives a Defender is some kind of emotional reaction. Its fears, resentments and longings determine what it does.

As you more and more deeply empathize with your Defenders, sensing what they are most dreading and longing for, they relax, too. Your Defenders let go of trying to do everything. You will find yourself doing what needs to be done with ease and flow. Your actions will come more and more into alignment with your unique strengths, values and interests, as you engage with the world and the challenges you meet.

The talents and strengths your Defenders have developed during your life become your talents and strengths, as Defenders melt back into your whole being.

Small Ones

How do Small Ones change? As you create a space where you can meet them in just the way they need, Small Ones no longer hide themselves away or sneak out when no one is looking to try and get what they feel they need.

In time, a Small One will trust you not to shame it for being how it is. In that climate of gentle, respectful, caring attention it is able to reveal itself more and more until it is fully received, fully known. As you hold a Small One in your compassionate embrace, you are able to experience what was impossible to feel and know when it first formed. Simply. Without drama.

What had been experienced as an eternal moment of horror or pain, loss or betrayal now lives within the context of your whole life. It is now done, over with, lived through, and gone beyond. Not abandoned or forgotten, but also not shackling you to the past.

The authentic, unique expression of who you are becomes possible. There's no longer a Small One at all. Simply you, living forward as your whole self.

Stoppages

Ever since the Stoppage occurred, the naturally arising next steps of life have not been possible. The Stoppage is how your body has continued to carry that stopped process. The next steps of life are embedded in it, like a seed, but they haven't yet had the conditions they needed to sprout, take root, and grow.

Part Four: Living Free

When you sense a Stoppage from Self-in-Presence, you are able to sense and embody the potential life held within the Stoppage. Your body knows how to live forward from there. What should have been possible then becomes possible now.

As you are sensing and symbolizing the felt sense of the Stoppage, it can make a quantum shift. Living forward can begin again immediately.

How that will show up in your life is not something anyone can tell in advance. Yet the quality of that living is unmistakable. You breathe differently and move more freely. You are more here. There is more of you engaged in life. And what was impossibly stuck in your life—is simply no more.

Going deep and going wide

Through doing Untangling, over time you will develop many abilities. The more your abilities strengthen, the more Untangling becomes possible for you. For example, you may be able to be present for very young Parts of you who are deeply in pain without shutting down or searching for distractions. Ironically, this can mean that you feel temporarily more uncomfortable than before. You might find yourself saying, "I've changed, and now I feel worse!" Yes... because you are stronger and can stand it.

Developing the five Powers of Presence makes it possible for you to go deep enough and wide enough to include whatever needs your attention in a Tangle. Whenever you widen your awareness to include another Part, you are moving horizontally to create a welcoming space where everything can come and be known. As you sense a Part's deep fears, you move vertically down to the bedrock of your being. As you sense its longings, you reach up to its dreams and visions.

As you move horizontally and vertically, you become a spacious, welcoming environment. Going deep and going wide creates the largest space where transformation occurs.

What transformation makes possible: Your unique life, lived more freely and fully, in all its infinite variety.

Chapter 20
LIVING BEYOND TANGLES

When Adam started learning Untangling, he was in his early forties. He'd been in various types of therapy and emotional healing for many years to try to get past the trauma of his early life. He'd had a physically and mentally abusive father, and a mother who was unable to protect him from that abuse. His own marriage had recently ended in divorce—partly, he felt, because of those early traumas. He had big dreams for the kind of life he wanted to create for himself, but he would often be consumed with frustration, anger, and sadness at the limitations he carried from the damage of his early years.

Adam moved to a city far away from his parents and rarely visited them. He rented a studio and pursued his dream of becoming a coach for actors and other performers. But it wasn't easy. Inner voices said things like, "How dare you create your own life!" and "Who do you think you are?" Sometimes, just as he would start to feel things were going well, he would be overcome with confusion and blankness or feel like he was hitting an invisible wall.

Slowly, Adam got better at cultivating Self-in-Presence and turning toward the Parts that arose as he created his new life. He was able to give Deep Empathy to the Protectors who create confusion and blankness, and discovered they were trying to protect him from feeling pain, terror, and hopelessness. He spent time with Defenders as well and was able to create a gentle relationship with the Small One the other Parts were guarding. That Small One still felt like a little boy terrified of a father who could snap into a violent rage with no warning. Adam was able to give tender empathy to that younger one inside him and to feel it start to respond to him in a softer and more trusting way.

At the heart of it all was a Stoppage where nothing moved, where love and connection seemed impossible. Adam was able to sense and describe and be with that Stoppage.

Although many things in his life had gotten easier, Adam didn't have any hopeful expectations about his long-delayed trip to see his parents. He

Part Four: Living Free

was anticipating and preparing for the usual: Parts getting triggered, his getting swamped with feeling angry or sad or anxious. He even decided to start smoking again during his stay because he thought it might give him a buffer from the emotional turmoil he was expecting.

What he actually experienced was very different from what he had imagined. Adam remained in Self-in-Presence most of the time around his parents, without any effort. He enjoyed himself so much that he even decided to stay for an extra week. He was taken completely by surprise at the calm freedom he felt. No smoking needed!

He realized that until recently his younger self had wanted so badly to get something from his parents, to hear "I'm sorry" or to receive some kind of acknowledgment of how it had been for him. What changed was that his Parts had finally received what they always needed—not from his parents but from *him*.

Adam wrote to us: "My Parts know they can rely on *my* presence, so there's no need to look outward. A part of me was doubtful if that place in me that was betrayed and violated so deeply by my father could be healed at all, but now I see it's possible, because it happened. Remarkable!"

Shift happens

As we have said, when a Tangle shifts, everything in your life connected with that Tangle shifts. It's hard to describe precisely what this means or how it will manifest, because it's different for each person.

One thing we can say, though: When you Untangle it will not look like you thought it would from inside your Tangle. Your Parts think they know what being untangled will be like. Your desk will be uncluttered and organized. You will exercise regularly and cheerfully. You will no longer fight with your nearest and dearest. You will be blissfully happy all the time. Okay, maybe your Parts never thought that, but you get the point.

But that kind of outcome is narrow. Even if you do get your desk cleared off and you exercise every day, those kinds of results are tiny, a drop in the bucket compared to what living an untangled life can actually be like.

What happens is so much more than you imagined when you were Tangled that the original desired goal can come to seem unimportant. You live more freely in all sorts of ways you would never have predicted. What we can predict is that what you thought was the problem will either become insignificant or that whole area of your life, including and exceeding the original problem, will be transformed beyond all recognition. You will live in a bigger, wider, freer world, whatever happens.

Here are a few stories from our students about what can happen when Tangles shift.

"Following my routines now sets me free"

Kay's Tangle was about how hard it was to maintain her routines—healthy eating, regular exercise, daily meditation. When she didn't stick to her routines, she felt guilty, like she was falling down in her responsibility to herself and her loved ones. But if she stayed with her routines, it didn't take long for her to feel suffocated, controlled, resentful, and restless. Both choices felt bad.

Kay had many goals for herself: weight-loss, meditation, tracking her finances—but she never managed to follow through on any of them. She felt frustrated, sad, disgusted with herself, and like a failure.

The Power of And helped her create a space for Parts of her that were in conflict: "Something in me wants to follow a consistent routine to reach my goals *and* something in me feels trapped by routines."

When she turned toward the Part that wanted her to be consistent, it told her that lack of consistency had ruined her life. It had a stern, scolding quality. When she turned toward the Part of her that failed to follow through on her goals, it felt rebellious and resistant, determined not to be controlled, not to give up any freedom.

The Power of Deep Empathy enabled Kay to connect with what both of these Parts were worried about and longing to help her with. It was especially important to hear what her rebellious Part was deeply Wanting for her: freedom! It wanted the exhilarating body feeling of aliveness that freedom brings.

At the end of that Untangling session, Kay felt at peace with the whole issue of her Tangle for the first time. She didn't know what would happen, but she felt open and curious.

Soon after that shift occurred, Kay found herself arranging to spend a day at the BMW Racing School—something completely at odds with her notion of her quiet 55-year-old self! She spent the whole day driving fast cars and learning about racing. She had a blast. It opened up whole new vistas for what could happen when she dared to try new things.

A few weeks later, Kay realized that without any apparent effort she had been exercising daily. The feeling of being trapped and tormented by rigid routine just wasn't there any more. She told us: "Rather than my daily routine being the enemy of my freedom, it has become clear that achieving my goals takes me toward a whole bigger freedom of physical wellness and strength."

"I'm now comfortable expressing myself in public"

Perhaps you remember Laurence and his Tangle about any kind of public speaking. If he dared to speak in front of others, especially when he was expressing his own ideas, he would be overcome with shame for days afterward. If he could not force himself to speak, he would accuse himself of being a coward and feel ashamed about that.

As his Protectors and Defenders calmed down and began to trust him, Laurence was able to get in touch with a Small One. It was like a young boy who felt completely excluded, stigmatized, and ostracized. Laurence said to that younger Part of himself, "I really get how hard that was, and still is, for you, to be rejected and alone." He could feel the Small One starting to trust in his presence.

Over time, Laurence began to feel his self-confidence growing. During one of his Untangling sessions, the image came to him of a deep-rooted fig tree basking in sunlight. There was a sense of his growth being nurtured. It felt like he was taking the time to be the gardener for his own writing and speaking. This felt deeply right.

In working with Untangling, Laurence realized that the Tangle was about much more than speaking in public. It was about any kind of expressive creativity. It was about sharing his unique take on things with others.

One day, in a writing group, Laurence found himself speaking without self-consciousness about how much he loved writing. He didn't realize it was happening until he looked around the room and saw people smiling at him, tears gleaming in some of their eyes.

"I did it," he told us, "and I didn't even know I was doing it."

"The easiest thing in the world"

Daisy is a talented artist who had won awards for her art when she was younger. But as she moved into her 30s and 40s, Daisy stopped painting. Her ability to practice her art became swallowed up by a Tangle.

As usual in Tangles, many worthwhile things she tried didn't help. She dedicated a spare room in her house as a studio... she filled it with art supplies... but she never actually drew or painted anything. Years went by.

When Daisy started working with us, she realized that it was a Defender Part of her that wasn't setting foot in the studio. And she discovered she had crowds of Protectors, both putting her down ("You're damaged") and trying to help her with various strategies such as "Just go in the studio for five minutes, that's all you have to do."

After cultivating Self-in-Presence, Daisy sensed many Parts entangled with each other. She created a wide welcome for all of them with *The Power of And*. She sensed "something in me that is keeping me away from painting" and "something in me that feels hopeless about this ever changing" as well as a number of other Parts. She was able to listen empathically to the fears and longings of each of these Parts.

In one Untangling session the Part that was keeping her away from painting was a little guy in armor just four inches high. In another session, the barrier to painting freely was a mountain, and inside a cave in the mountain was a little girl busy with art supplies.

Spending time with Parts like these in session after session, Daisy began to feel a sense of possibility growing. She sensed she was close to a transformation of some kind.

After about seven sessions like these, Daisy found herself setting up her easel on her sunny porch.

In her own words, here is what happened next: "My husband just sat at a table, and I painted him. It was so easy. It was the first time I had sat at my easel in ten years, but it was just so normal. The next day we did it again, and the next day. Then I went on a trip, and on the trip I started sketching. When I came back, the easel came out again.

"What amazes me most of all is that it was just so ordinary. No trumpets playing! The easiest thing in the world. I would say it's like magic, and it was, but it was also so normal. That's the weirdest part! I could have been getting something out of the fridge, that's how normal it was."

Barbara and Ann

We have the longest history with Untangling... over twenty-five years. What has happened in our lives is both remarkable and mundane. We are learning, growing human beings who still have areas of our lives that don't flow as freely as they could. And our lives have become so much freer in so many ways. Perhaps most importantly, we are much more able to respond quickly when something needs our attention.

Our ability to collaborate with each other, which has evolved through challenges of many kinds, continues to develop and grow. How we each appear has changed dramatically, in terms of our weight, the clothes we wear, our relaxed presence in public settings.

One way our lives have changed dramatically is in the quality of our closest relationships: Ann with Joe, Barbara with John and Sara. These relationships continue to be sources of support, pleasure, discovery, and love... as well as challenge and learning!

Important as these are, they are still insignificant details compared to the inner shifts that have occurred.

>**BARBARA:** One of the biggest changes for me has been a massive shift in what I call my baseline. When I first learned Focusing and even ten years later when Ann and I started working together, it wouldn't take much to "knock me off my perch." I would easily feel I had done something wrong, I was stupid, I should have known better—and I would feel terrible about it. I would plunge into a dark pit of depression and despair. I was anxious a lot of the time. It felt like a burning in my stomach which went from mild heat to scorching during every day. It was constant and it wore me out.
>
>There have been thousands of shifts over the years through hundreds of Untangling sessions. I can't say that any single shift is what made a difference in how I now feel, though there have been a few magnificently memorable ones. My stomach is now happy and calm most of the time, and when it isn't, I know something needs my attention.

A big change is how I am now able to hear feedback with curiosity and openness. I can hear whatever someone says to me without thinking I'm a terrible, useless failure.

In other words, I am now resilient. When something in life is just a little too challenging to deal with easily, I can slow down. Sometimes I need to turn toward a Part that is trying to take care of the situation and I can do that from a calm, clear, spacious Presence.

Food is no longer a source of shame and conflict. I am able to make considered choices about what I eat without struggle or fuss. It's easy—well, most of the time. And when it isn't, I am able to notice what's going on. Usually it means I have not been taking care of myself in some other way.

I have learned how to be kind to myself: gentle, caring, patient. And I believe this has made it possible for me to be kinder and more gentle and patient with others. My relationships are closer and more real than ever before, and that is hugely precious to me. And, of course, this is a lifelong process of living more deeply, authentically and fully.

ANN: My life before Untangling, and even many years into doing the work, was marked by denial and unconsciousness. Unlike Barbara, I was not aware of being depressed or of having painful feelings in my body. Instead, I acted out my Tangle, through drinking, smoking marijuana, having unrealistic romantic fantasies, and being insensitive in my relationships.

As an example of the latter, when my younger brother went away to college, I never wrote to him or called him. I knew he was lonely. I just couldn't or didn't call him. Many years later, after his children were born, I did little to get to know them. There was no family rift. I simply didn't do it. I'll never get back the years of relationship I missed with my brother and my nieces because of my Tangle.

All of those symptoms and consequences, I now know, stemmed from a Small One who was trying to get what she was missing, complicated by the strategies of Protectors and Defenders doing their best to keep me from feeling unbearably painful feelings.

What is life like now? I feel present to myself. I can and do turn toward anxious or sad or other hard feelings and include them.

I have no need for behaviors that distract me from feelings. It is no trouble at all to avoid alcohol and other inebriants... and a few years ago I easily stopped eating sugar.

I no longer get "crushes" or become romantically obsessed with people. And what a relief that is... for me and for my friends! I have great relationships with my nieces and nephews now, and with their kids. When my foster daughter became a single mom and invited me to be a grandmother, I joyfully stepped into the give-and-take of that fulfilling and important relationship.

My heart is much more available for caring and compassion in relationships of all kinds, including with my students and clients.

My willingness to feel fear and discomfort makes it possible to do scary things that I always wanted to do but didn't dare, such as putting myself on larger stages for public speaking. At the same time, I know my worth doesn't depend on how much I achieve or how well-known I am. I am deeply satisfied with my life as it is. It is not just enough, it is plenty!

When your Parts become you

As your Tangle begins to untangle, the abilities, strengths, skills and competencies that your Parts have developed over the years to cope with your Tangle are free to be used in creative and life-enhancing ways throughout all areas of your life.

When a Tangle untangles, your Parts' strategies become unhooked from it. They become freed from the repertoire of a Part and simply become another possible way for you to do something. You go for a walk because you choose to, not because it is something you should do. You take in feedback because you want to learn, not because there's something fundamentally wrong with you and you need to shape up. You do things for others because you care about them, not because you have to do it to be a "good person."

Untangled, you make choices from a different place. You make choices from you as a whole. And this needn't be a conscious, "I am choosing" kind of place. You might simply find yourself making a difficult phone call or tracking your food or getting out the door for a walk or writing a book or reaching out to help a friend. No struggle. No shame. No "should." Just doing it.

Free — even when Parts still exist

Untangling means that you are bigger, more present, more available, more alive. It doesn't mean your Parts have to disappear. Your Parts might become less active, naturally fading and melting into your larger being. But they don't even have to do that for huge changes to occur.

Parts do not have to change for us to be able to live differently.

Parts can be as they are. The idea that Parts must change in order for change to happen is an old idea, a limited idea. It comes from that earlier world of yours in which there were only Parts. In a world in which you are Self-in-Presence, there is actually no need for Parts to change.

For example, perhaps you have realized that the reason you are not writing the book you've always longed to write is that there is a Protector Part anxiously pushing you to do it and a Defender Part that resents being driven. The Defender Part is the one not doing the writing.

It's easy to think that what needs to happen here is for the Protector Part to back off and the Defender Part to feel good about getting back to the manuscript. You might think it would help to ask, "What does that Part need in order to be able to write?" But no! Here's the thing we want to make clear: It won't be the Defender Part that writes. It will be you who either writes — or freely chooses not to write!

You will probably find yourself writing while there are still Parts running around, with more healing and transforming still to come. Or you may find yourself realizing that you don't actually want to write. You want to do something else you had never thought possible before.

You will probably always have some Parts, but they don't have to be running your life. You can be a loving Presence where the Parts in your Tangle can be felt, known, and acknowledged — and you can act as your freer, larger Self.

Part Four: Living Free

A lifelong way of being

Because life is process, there is always something next. As you live beyond Tangles you naturally live more and more freely and easily. This includes simply getting on with the day-to-day tasks of life. You are more able to meet the inevitable challenges life throws at you, with curiosity and patience and courage.

If you stop to notice, you will probably recognize how certain experiences that may have once been all too common have now melted away: anxiously avoiding situations, being tense and driven to accomplish, feeling despairing, frustrated, and discouraged about ever reaching your goals. Those feelings may have colored your daily life, from brushing your teeth to going after your biggest dreams. Tangles affect our whole lives.

As your Tangles resolve, they will take up less and less space in your life. The leftover bits of them will be more and more like little knots you encounter in the smooth skein of living. Living from Self-in-Presence more and more enables you to turn toward what needs your attention, even when it is painful or difficult.

What is a lifelong way of being Untangled? It comes down to this: Living from Self-in-Presence is both something you intentionally practice and cultivate, and an effortless way of living.

The Powers of Presence in an Untangling life

Here are some of the ways you can continue to develop and strengthen the Powers of Presence for the rest of your life.

The Power of Cultivating Self-in-Presence

Developing the habit of *Resourcing* will help you to maintain your strength so you can meet the challenges that life presents. It will help you recharge your batteries and bring pleasure and joy into your daily life.

Developing the ability of *Recognizing* will help you notice when you are merging with a Part. It will help you pause and re-establish Self-in-Presence so you can act from your largest self in the flow of your life.

Developing the capacity of *Relating* will help you be able to turn toward your Parts with curiosity and be compassionate to what they are feeling.

You'll be able to do this with other people as well, even when they are merged with *their* Parts.

The Power of And

Developing *The Power of And* will help you to widen your awareness to include and welcome whatever needs attention in any situation. You will be able to hold divergent points of view between your Parts without needing to force a conclusion. Your capacity to acknowledge and welcome the differing viewpoints of other people will also expand.

The Power of Deep Empathy

As you strengthen your capacity for *Deep Empathy*, you become confident that there is always some understandable motivation even behind Parts that seem harsh or destructive, and that in relationship with you, such Parts inevitably change. This changes your empathy for other people's deeper motivations as well.

The Power of Felt-Sensing the Stoppage

There are lots of interruptions in the flow of life. Once you have developed your ability for *Felt-Sensing a Stoppage,* you can directly sense how your body has a disruption in your life as it is happening. You can pause and sense what it is like.

When you find the metaphor (the image, the word or phrase, the gesture) that fits what it feels like in your body at that moment, this "pausing and sensing" allows what could become a Stoppage to become a source of energy and creativity instead.

The Power of Felt-Sensing It All

There will always be situations in your life you don't yet know how to deal with. As you develop *The Power of Felt-Sensing It All,* you will feel more and more confident in inviting a felt sense of the whole thing.

You will become comfortable inviting everything that is relevant in this situation to be summed up by your body. You will be able to lean into the space where something new can emerge.

When you invite a felt sense of the whole thing in this way, you are inviting the situation to take its next step. Each time you get a felt sense of a situation, you are developing your capacity to trust in the ongoing process of life living forward. When you are in alignment with that process, the life force within you will pick you up and carry you into the next right steps of life.

Living free

How does it feel to live your life from Self-in-Presence, more and more of the time?

Tom described it this way: "The past days, working on my presentation, I often practiced coming into Self-in-Presence, which allowed a sense of calm to come in relation to my project. I have been reveling in the body-knowing that it will take time, and progress will be slow, and that's okay. This is so different from the usual critical voice inside warning, 'You'd better hurry up; you'll never get it done.'"

Felicity told us: "Yesterday I had the best day with my sister in all of our adult lives. Nearly forty years. We were engaged, connected. The conversation was exciting, spilling over, and we were really listening to each other. That level of connection had not seemed possible even a week ago. And the best part—I didn't plan it or try to manage it. I wasn't trying to be Self-in-Presence. It just happened."

Companions on the journey of life

In a Tangle, we are isolated and alone. As we get free of our Tangles, we know ourselves to be vibrant threads in a tapestry to which we contribute and from which we receive.

You are always part of the vastly complex and intricate system of the living world. Your relationships with other people, animals, and all of nature are essential to being who you are. They are not "extra."

If life is a journey, you are never without companions on that journey. We would like to invite you to pause and in the words of Mister Rogers: "Would you just take, along with me, ten seconds to think of the people who have helped you become who you are....Ten seconds of silence."

Know who you are and remember you are never alone.

Ripples

We have a vision of what is possible from living an Untangling life. As we Untangle and are more able to live our own free life, this has unknowable effects that ripple out into the world in unforeseeable ways.

We believe every moment you live from Self-in-Presence contributes to a world that is congruent with the deepest stream of life. Not caught up in the desperate push and pull of your Parts, you can tap into larger rhythms and act, when possible, in harmony with the greatest good for all.

Life is fraught with challenges, and we will often stumble. It is not about how many times you fail to live from Self-in-Presence... for you will. It is about how often you acknowledge what has happened and turn toward what needs attention, both within you and in others, with courageous caring and kind curiosity.

What's possible now?

Our brains are wired to notice difficulties rather than what's positive. We notice what's not possible more readily than what's possible. So at this point in your journey, we invite you to do something different and deliberately notice what is possible for you now in your Tangle.

Sometimes the answer seems like very little. Remember Ann's "I could go in a clothing store and be curious"? Yet when something is possible that wasn't possible before, even something tiny, that's a big deal—and you can celebrate. You are already living beyond what got stuck—and that makes so much more possible than you can know.

Sometimes the changes affect every aspect of life.

Barbara now greets the day, happy to be alive. She looks forward to discover what life will hold for her today. She no longer feels isolated and ashamed if she needs support. She knows she has deep and loving relationships with many people that she can call on when life feels too much for her to deal with on her own.

Ann's vibrancy and joy in life has grown fuller and fuller over the years. At the same time, she has become softer, kinder, more open to connecting with other people at a deep heart level. She's more generous toward "flaws" in herself and others, which of course don't even seem like flaws anymore. She sees her losses of abilities as her 70s advance as something to smile about rather than something to worry over.

Living fully is so much more than reaching goals or accumulating accomplishments. Living richly and deeply is interacting meaningfully with others and the world around you.

As you develop your Powers of Presence, you'll have many more resources for facing the difficulties and troubles that come at you, as they surely will. When Parts get triggered, you will know how to turn toward them with loving, compassionate attention.

When your Tangles untangle, you become more fully yourself, freed from what has limited and narrowed your responses to life. You will have more of what you need to be your own unique self. Vibrantly alive, feeling whole, comfortable in your own skin, living your own life.

There is always a next step to be taken and then another as life unfolds. So... *What's possible now that wasn't possible before?*

APPENDIX

Some Untangling terms
Some books that influenced us
Ways to go further
With Gratitude and Appreciation

Appendix

Some Untangling terms

Defender:

A type of Part that is typically impulsive, compulsive, overwhelmed, rebellious, disconnected, depressed, embarrassed, or ashamed. Defenders often appear as children or adolescents. Defenders have agency (can act in the world) and are usually non-verbal, emotional, and bodily felt, if they are felt at all. In Tangles, Defenders or Small Ones are the Parts taking action or refusing to act.

Empathy:

Empathy is "getting how it is" for someone. It is meeting them where they are, without judgement or analysis or advice. Just getting how it is for them: what they think and how they feel, what they are up against and how they are attempting to deal with that.

Felt Sense:

A direct experience of how your body has the whole of something. A felt sense comes when you pause and invite it. The forming of a felt sense allows the possibility of a quantum leap, something unexpected, a genuinely new resolution, something that cannot be predicted.

Focusing:

A research-based process of inner awareness in which open, accepting attention is brought to a felt sense of an issue, project, or situation. Focusing is used in a wide range of circumstances: for emotional healing, to enhance spirituality and creativity, to help ease the suffering of chronic pain and illness, and in many other areas of life.

Inner Relationship Focusing is an elaboration of Focusing that includes cultivating Self-in-Presence and developing relationships with Parts.

Merging:

Also called "being identified." Narrowing of awareness to the point of view of a Part. The experience of being a Part, including having its emotions, thoughts and beliefs. Responding to present-day situations from the narrow viewpoint of a Part.

Parts:

Repetitive and habitual reaction patterns that persist over time. Parts arise at a Stoppage. They are attempts by the organism to live past the Stoppage without the full resources needed to do so. They have individual points of view which include beliefs, fears and desires which may be quite different from the beliefs and fears held by other Parts.

Powers of Presence:

Cultivating Self-in-Presence: Whatever we do to cultivate the ability to turn toward any aspect of awareness, including Parts, with calm, compassion, and curiosity. Self-in-Presence is cultivated through Recognizing, Resourcing, and Relating.

And: The ability to hold more than one Part in awareness without becoming identified with any of them. This ability also includes the possibility of sensing multiple aspects of a situation simultaneously.

Deep Empathy: Giving an entangled Part the kind of empathy it needs to go beyond its strategies and defenses, judgements and impulses to what truly matters to it. Deep Empathy enables a Part to have its hopes and dreams received and heard, by you as Self-in-Presence.

Felt-Sensing the Stoppage: The process of getting a felt sense of the Stoppage at the core of a Tangle, symbolizing it, and staying with it until the symbol and the felt sense match each other and the felt sense shifts.

Felt-Sensing It All: The process of getting a felt sense of the whole of a Tangle (including the Parts, the situation, the human and circumstantial environment, both known and not-yet-known), and then allowing a symbol to emerge that matches the felt sense. This may include allowing a felt sense of the next forward steps to form.

Protector:

A type of Part that is typically blaming, critical, anxious, restrictive, pushing, hyper-alert, and worried about future consequences. A Protector has no agency (cannot act in the world), so must influence other Parts to act. It often appears as an inner voice (e.g., "You're hopeless") It can constrict your muscles, confuse your thoughts or make you feel nauseated.

Appendix

Recognizing:

Becoming aware that one is merged with a Part. Recognizing is the first step towards unmerging. Also becoming aware that more than one Part is involved in your Tangle, for example becoming aware you are merged with a Part that feels like it is under attack and then recognizing there is a second Part that is silently and invisibly attacking the first Part.

Relating:

Creating an empathic relationship with a Part. Self-in-Presence is the "I" relating to a Part.

Resourcing:

Strengthening the ability to be Self-in-Presence by embracing and enjoying nourishing, restorative experiences, and also remembering such experiences.

Self-in-Presence:

The ability to turn toward any and all Parts with compassion, curiosity, and empathy.

The ability to respond to present-time situations without being merged with Parts.

Small One:

A type of Part that carries the unchanged, not-completely-formed feelings from the Stoppage at the start of the Tangle. A Small One is is typically experienced as under or behind other Parts, or hidden, vague, or hard to feel. Small Ones are a kind of Defender, being able to take action in the world. If they appear human, they often seem to be very young children. Being merged with a Small One can be experienced as ecstatic devotion, utter despair, or excoriating rage.

Stoppage:

The ongoing experience of the forward momentum of life being stopped. Also called "stopped process," Stoppage contains both what is/was impossible and the potential for the flow of living to resume. Stoppage gives rise to Parts as attempts to get part of what was needed in some form.

Books that Have Influenced Us

There are many more books we could put in this list. Here are the ones that have been especially important to us as we've created our work.

Dweck, Carol.

Mindset: The New Psychology of Success. Ballantine Books, 2006

> Carol Dweck's understanding of the difference between a fixed and growth mindset has huge implications for learning, healing and transformational change.

Gendlin, Eugene.

Focusing. Bantam, 1982.

> Our debt to Gendlin is immeasurable. This little book is a good starting place for the powerful method that has changed millions of lives.

Focusing-Oriented Psychotherapy: A Manual of the Experiential Method. The Guilford Press, 1996

> Although this is a book on psychotherapy, it's also the most accessible book on Gendlin's philosophy. (Many of our favorite quotes come from here.) An inspiring and deeply hopeful book.

A Process Model. Northwestern University Press, 2017

> The existential phenomenological philosophy set out in this book underpins our work in Untangling. It details how living process implies its next step, how it can be interrupted and how it can recommence.

Hanson, Rick.

Resilient: How to Grow an Unshakable Core of Calm, Strength, and Happiness (with Forrest Hanson). Harmony, 2018.

> Rick Hanson gave us confirmation for our understanding that positive, enjoyable experiences are worth taking time with. His maxim "Take in the good!" is a wise reminder of one of the most important ways to cultivate Self-in-Presence.

Appendix

Levine, Peter.

In an Unspoken Voice: How the Body Releases Trauma and Restores Goodness North Atlantic Books, 2010.

Waking the Tiger North Atlantic Books, 1997.

Healing Trauma (tapes) Sounds True, 1999.

> Peter Levine's brilliant work on trauma—what it is and how it heals—contributed to our view of Defenders as fighting, fleeing, or freezing, and especially the idea that even freezing ("playing possum") is a survival strategy. Levine also contributed to our list of resources for Self-in-Presence—opening the eyes, looking around the room—and to the concept of "resourcing."

Schwartz, Richard C.

Internal Family Systems Therapy Guilford Publications, 1997.

> When we encountered Schwartz's work in 2004, we were surprised at how similar it was to ours. We learned a lot from his system. There are still important differences—he doesn't have the concept of the felt sense, and tends to treat parts as permanent—but we are grateful to him for the notion of Self which has agency and is capable of leadership, which broadened our understanding of Self-in-Presence. His insight that when the resources of Self get overwhelmed Parts take on extreme roles (in his system) was helpful in us understanding how Parts are formed (in our system). Also his formulation of three types of Parts, though not the same as ours, helped us to clarify what we had been observing.

Appendix

WAYS TO GO FURTHER

Here are some suggestions for training and practice for those who would like support in going further with Focusing and Untangling®.

Learn Inner Relationship Focusing

Learning Inner Relationship Focusing is the first step to making the Focusing process your own and bringing Untangling into your life.

Our Inner Relationship Focusing training program is called "Your Path to Lasting Change," or "Path" for short. This eighteen-week live online training is offered at Focusing Resources three times a year. It is also offered by approved graduates of our teacher training program.

In it, you will learn the stages of the Focusing process, and how to have a Focusing partnership, where two people exchange Focusing turns as peers. You will also learn fundamental Untangling practices such as: cultivating Self-in-Presence, and how to offer empathic company to Parts, as well as felt-sensing.

https://focusingresources.com/learning/your-path-to-lasting-change/

Attend an Untangling® Retreat

Once you complete the Path program or its equivalent with another Inner Relationship Focusing teacher, you are welcome to register for one of our Untangling® Retreats.

Taught in person by both of us together, these six-day retreats are a great opportunity to learn and practice the five powers of Presence by applying them to a current Tangle. You'll immerse yourself in the Untangling process in a friendly community setting, in a beautiful part of the world. Many people find Untangling partners during our retreats and go on to work together after the workshops finishes. Currently we are offering two retreats per year, one in Europe and one in North America, and others may be held in other areas of the world in the future.

We also offer an online Untangling Intensive so people who cannot travel can also participate in this work. It is held over six days on two consecutive weekends.

https://focusingresources.com/learning/untangling/

Appendix

Join Getting Free—a Year of Untangling®

Possibly the best way to make Untangling an integral part of your life is to join Getting Free, our yearlong online course. In twenty-four sessions taught by both of us, we take you step by step through cultivating the five Powers of Presence so you can engage with your Tangle in ways that enable it to release. This partnership course is open to graduates of the Path program or its equivalent.

https://focusingresources.com/learning/getting-free-a-year-of-untangling/

Work with an Inner Relationship Focusing Practitioner

You may want to have more support and focused attention than you can get working on your own or with an Untangling Partner. Having sessions with a Focusing Practitioner can help.

A Focusing Practitioner is not a therapist. The focus of their work is to help you in strengthening your Powers of Presence so you can offer your Parts the kind of company they need.

At the time of writing this, Ann and Barbara have only a few places available for working with people individually. A directory of recommended Inner Relationship Focusing Practitioners can be found at:

https://focusingresources.com/find-a-focusing-teacher/

Other Resources

There are many courses available at Focusing Resources from entry level on-demand courses to advanced courses for experienced Focusers and helping professionals.

https://focusingresources.com/workshop_calendar/

There is also a free library of articles, blogs and videos for you to peruse.

https://focusingresources.com/our-library/

Something you could do for us—and future readers

Of course, we deeply appreciate reviews on Amazon or Goodreads, and, just as importantly, they help other readers, like yourself, to find books that help shape their lives. Will you take a moment to leave a review, or share on your socials what this book has meant to you? We thank you from the bottom of our hearts.

Appendix

WITH GRATITUDE AND APPRECIATION

Countless people helped us with this book, and we are enormously grateful. We wish we could name all of you individually, but we have to settle for thanking you all, and naming a few.

We treasure all our wonderful students and assistants, in particular the people who agreed to having their stories included in this book. We have learned so much from you. Thank you for your courage, your vulnerability, your trust in us.

Our deepest gratitude to our dear friend Marcella Calabi. Among many astute observations, she contributed the important insight that Recognizing is one of the three essential "R's" of cultivating Self-in-Presence.

An expert editor, Marcella read through three complete drafts of this book in detail, spotting the places where we needed to rethink, reorganize, simplify and clarify what we were trying to convey. Her depth of thought inspired us to have the courage to completely reorganize the book between versions.

Marcella is a person who thinks deeply and expresses herself with extraordinary clarity. Her own business is called Clarityworks, www.clarityworks.net, and we highly recommend her.

We're deeply grateful to these people who read and commented on an early draft: Elizabeth Kaye, Terri Thayer, and Lucinda Hayden. Their insightful comments have helped make this a much better and clearer book.

Deep bows to those who read and commented on our final draft, spotting everything from major problems to tiny typos: Shannon Crossman, Jinevra Howard, Allison Jones, Jacek Kaleta, Hope Maltz, Joseph McBride, and Judy Schavrien.

Sachne Kilner took one last editing pass through the book to make sure all the bits are in the right place. Any mistakes that remain are totally ours.

Much appreciation to Alberto Hernandez, our excellent sound engineer for the audiobook.

Appendix

Endless gratitude to the staff at Focusing Resources for all of their support. Shannon Crossman, Maggie Hurley, Allison Jones, and Isabella Canal are a team without equal. Knowing we could rely on them to keep the Focusing Resources ship moving forward allowed us to be able to concentrate on getting this book finally written. We especially want to acknowledge Maggie's invaluable expertise in graphic design and book production and Shannon's knowledge of how to get the book into your hands.

And finally, our closest families—Barbara's daughter Sara and husband John, and Ann's partner Joe, daughter Mika, and granddaughter Isabelle—whose loving support sustains us, and was one of the main contributions that enabled us to write a book that took 29 years to complete.

Barbara McGavin, Bath, England, and Sacramento, California

Ann Weiser Cornell, Berkeley, California

August 2024

Ann Weiser Cornell   Barbara McGavin

Who we are

Barbara McGavin and *Ann Weiser Cornell* have been friends since 1983. In 1994 their teaching partnership took a big leap when together they began discovering the processes of change that became Untangling®. Since then they've had the pleasure of offering Untangling® retreats and online classes for people seeking transformation all over the world. They are also the co-developers of Inner Relationship Focusing.

Barbara has a background in humanistic psychology, teaching, fine art, and graphic design. Ann has a background in linguistics and humanistic psychology. They both love reading and knitting.

Barbara divides her time between Bath, England, and Citrus Heights, California. Ann lives in Berkeley, California.

Advance Praise for *Untangling*

"*Untangling* is a path of profound transformation that can bring healing to even our most deep and stuck places. The authors introduce accessible, potent practices through their own personal and compelling stories, a pioneering and brilliant use of language, and most important, their thorough, inside-out wisdom as to what enables authentic inner freedom. Highly recommended!"

—*Tara Brach,*
Author of Radical Acceptance

"Every once in a while, I discover a modality that is grounded in the teachings of Eugene Gendlin, whose work is a basis for many somatic practices. This book provides valuable support to becoming a more whole, vital you. Untangling, developed by Barbara McGavin and Ann Weiser Cornell, is a transformative somatic method that enables us to cultivate healing through empathy and by attuning to our bodies through the felt-sense. Using this method, we can begin to heal our relationship to ourselves, in an embodied way, and can transform our connection to self, others, and our world. Untangling is a path well worth exploring."

—*Peter Levine,*
author of *In an Unspoken Voice* and *Waking the Tiger*
and founder of *Somatic Experiencing International*

"From two luminaries carrying forward the lineage of Focusing comes a masterwork decades in the making. Untangling reveals their hard-won secrets for resolving inner conflict—honed through years of exploration, tears and triumph. Through stories, examples, and step-by-step guidance, master teachers Barbara McGavin and Ann Weiser Cornell reveal how to become 'Self-in-Presence'—a calm yet courageous space for your inner parts to relax and release.

"At last, the missing piece that unlocks stuck places from the inside out. Their method marries science and spirit, rigor and heart. With wisdom and wit, they guide you through tangled territory to uncover hidden wholeness. Come witness the strange alchemy—how life's impasses transform into flow. How the fragmented self awakens to joyful presence. A living testament to the incredible resilience of the human spirit. Start untangling what feels impossibly stuck. Discover the freedom, joy and authenticity you long for. This trailblazing book points the way."

—*Albert Wong, Ph.D.,*
Director of the Trauma Certificate Program at Somatopia
and author of *The Healing Trauma Workbook*

"What a gem! Ann and Barbara's book, *Untangling*, offers us both understanding and action for one of life's messiest puzzles—how to resolve hopelessly entrenched problems we struggle with on a daily basis. Untangling gracefully guides us towards insights about why we do things that we then criticize ourselves for and feel helpless to do differently. By seeing the 'doing' and the 'criticizing' and the 'helpless' as parts of ourselves that all need empathic regard and embodied presence, and by being with all these parts as they are, we uncover their stories. And their stories always, at the heart of it, involve motivations to keep us safe and whole. By welcoming and integrating our various parts, we untangle a knot of seemingly oppositional strands into a coherent weave, a tapestry of creative wholeness.

"What makes this book unique and deeply contributive is its accessibility. Ann and Barbara have used their own stories of struggle as a means of showing us how tangles form and sustain themselves. Their honest and courageous personal stories are relatable and immediately rolled over into approaches that start and then sustain the untangling process. In the midst of reading this book, we can find ourselves empowered and resourced for working through our own most stubborn tangles. I suspect that many of us will keep this book close and use it frequently, as it so simply and gracefully addresses such core life experiences."

—*Christine Caldwell, Ph.D., LPC, BC-DMT*
Professor Emeritus, Naropa University Somatic Counseling Program
author of *Bodyfulness*

"This gem of a book brings the authors' clear and evocative writing to their work extending Inner Relationship Focusing to more complex processes of stuckness ('tangles') among parts or aspects of self, including a range of key psychological difficulties such as depression, substance misuse and anxiety difficulties. Person-centered therapists and counselors will resonate with the emphasis on deep empathy, listening patiently, and being open to all aspects of experience. Emotion-Focused Therapists will immediately see the usefulness of Barbara and Ann's formulations and practices for various kinds of chair work, both as an alternative and as a way of deepening that work. I've already highlighted large sections of this lovely book. Highly recommended."

Robert Elliott, Ph.D.,
co-originator of Emotion Focused Therapy,
co-author of *Emotion Focused Therapy in Action*
and *Learning Emotion Focused Therapy*

"*Untangling* is an easy-reading, yet superb self-help guide that equips lay readers with some of the most effective methods of focused, experiential psychotherapy—and that is no small achievement! The process of inner self-discovery and transformational change mapped out in this book will be truly liberating for innumerable people."

—Bruce Ecker, LMFT,
co-director, Coherence Psychology Institute, co-originator of Coherence Therapy, and co-author of *Unlocking the Emotional Brain*

"Barbara and Ann have written an insightful and compassionate guide for working with life's most difficult challenges. Drawing on deeply personal and intimate experience, coupled with years of study and inquiry, Untangling offers insight and practical tools for anyone attempting to break free from their limitations and unhelpful patterns. This book is for anyone seeking to shift from 'stuckness' and move into a place of transformation and flow."

—Dr. Scott Lyons,
holistic psychologist, mind-body medicine specialist,
founder of The Embody Lab, and author of *Addicted to Drama*

McGavin and Cornell's wonderful book *Untangling* offers a different way of approaching "parts" work from an embodied inner relationship stance. Studded with illuminating stories from the authors' personal lives, *Untangling* offers stunning insights into the structure of our knottiest and most intractable inner conflicts, and shows readers the way out—by deeply listening with compassion to the hidden and exiled parts of the self that are waiting to be heard and understood. *Untangling* will be invaluable for psychotherapists and laypeople alike who are seeking a method for working through difficult and deep-seated emotional issues and blocks.

Helene G. Brenner, Ph.D.,
Focusing Oriented Therapist
and author of *I Know I'm in There Somewhere*

"A brilliantly supportive, generous, and life giving book. Ann and Barbara offer themselves and their work to support people on how to meet difficult and stuck places with a method that is filled with presence, love, and compassion. The stories, examples, and guidance bring life to this work, and the possibility of staying close to life's own unfolding."

—Cynthia Luna,
Managing Partner at New Ventures West
and Co-founder of Praxsys Leadership

"The very concept of untangling is profound and transformative. Ann and Barbara zero in on the stuck places and self-destructive thoughts and behaviors that seem impossible to change. This book shows you, with vivid examples and brave self-disclosure, how to actually untangle those tangles. We have both personally experienced the amazing work that Ann and Barbara do and it has deeply influenced both our personal lives and our work on healing shame. As they say, 'When your Tangle shifts, everything shifts.' Untangling provides a map to a freer and more interesting life that is brilliant, inviting, and amazingly practical. This book can change your life."

—*Sheila Rubin, LMFT* and *Bret Lyon, Ph.D.*,
authors of *Embracing Shame*
and co-directors of the Center for Healing Shame